GHOSTS OF SU

GHOSTS
OF
SUFFOLK

Betty Puttick

COUNTRYSIDE BOOKS
NEWBURY, BERKSHIRE

First published 1998
© Betty Puttick 1998
Reprinted 2004, 2011

Countryside Books
3 Catherine Road
Newbury, Berkshire

To view our complete range of books,
please visit us at
www.countrysidebooks.co.uk

ISBN 978 1 85306 518 7

Cover illustration by Colin Doggett
Map by Trevor Yorke

Produced through MRM Associates Ltd., Reading
Typeset by Acorn Bookwork, Salisbury
Printed by Information Press, Oxford

Contents

Introduction   11

1. What's in a Name?   13

2. The Ghost with the Christmas Post   19

3. The Rougham Mirage   23

4. A Dream of Murder   30

5. The Strange Story of Corder's Skull   37

6. Ghosts of the Highways and Byways   42

7. The Return of Henrietta   46

8. The Haunt of the Black Dog   50

9. The Phantom Fliers   55

10. Bury's Ghostly Monks and Others   61

11. Trouble at the Mill   64

12. Strange Visitors   68

13. The Mystery of the Bells   76

14. Ghosts Galore   81

15. Supernatural Walberswick and Neighbourhood   91

16. The City that Drowned   98

17. Murder on the *Mayfly*   102

18. Strange Discoveries   106

19. Monks in the Market   109

20. Do You Believe in Fairises?   112

21. Haunted Inns   115

22. The Unknown Bride   121

All houses wherein men have lived and died
Are haunted houses. Through the open doors
The harmless phantoms on their errands glide,
With feet that make no sound upon the floors.

Henry Wadsworth Longfellow

Let us enjoy our ghosts. They were here first.

James Wentworth Day

GHOSTS OF SUFFOLK

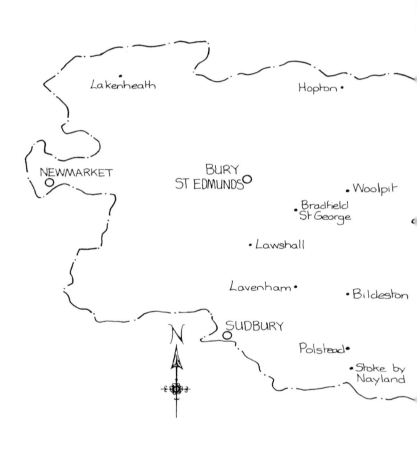

Lakenheath

Hopton •

NEWMARKET

BURY
ST EDMUNDS

• Woolpit

• Bradfield
St George

• Lawshall

Lavenham •

• Bildeston

N

SUDBURY

Polstead •

• Stoke by
Nayland

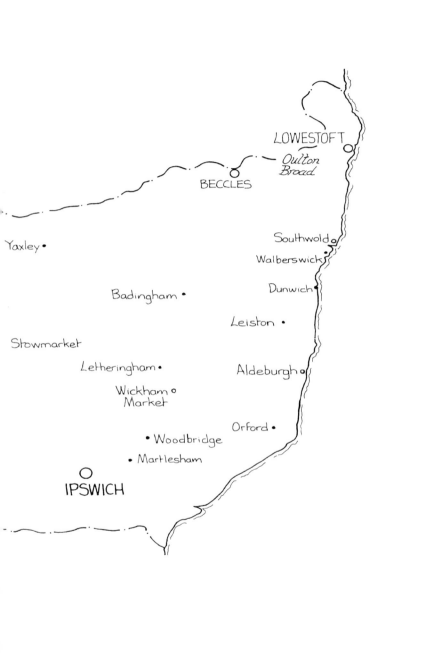

Acknowledgements

My grateful thanks to everyone who took the time and trouble to help me with my enquiries, especially Wesley H. Downes, Bryan Hall, Pete Jennings, Paul Kemp and Edna Simms.

Introduction

SUFFOLK has many strange and unusual stories which is not surprising as it is a unique county. When you visit some of its quiet places sometimes it seems like stepping back in time, and yet if you did, you would find a different Suffolk with a very turbulent history.

Suffolk has been frequently invaded by both men and Nature. Romans, Saxons, Danes and Normans have left their mark in many ways, but perhaps the greatest invader was the stormy sea which savaged the coastline and devastated thriving ports and splendid cities.

But Suffolk is still beautiful with its wide skies and a light that painters from Constable down to the most amateur weekend dabbler find an inspiration.

I have discovered a treasure trove of stories and legends of wild men, green children, even a cousin of the Loch Ness Monster, the Kessingland serpent! That alarming dog of darkness Black Shuck ranges throughout East Anglia and is well-known in Suffolk, and another monster, Matthew Hopkins, the 17th-century Witchfinder General, also had Suffolk in his sights as he pursued his ruthless vendetta against witches throughout East Anglia. And yet he didn't eradicate them all, as some of the stories I found suggest.

There are bells that once rang of their own accord, and bells that still chime although their church towers are deep below the sea, and all kinds of ghosts, including my favourites, Henrietta who haunts wherever her portrait goes and a mysterious house that appears, phantom-like, and vanishes as if it had never been. There are grey ladies, silver ladies, a tragic phantom bride and monks galore.

Most ghoulish of all is a haunted gibbet with an apparition fit for the most terrifying Hammer Horror movie. These are just some of Suffolk's spooks and spectres, and there are many more.

Interest in every aspect of the paranormal is very strong these days, and whereas people who experienced a brush with the supernatural once kept quiet about it lest they should be dubbed a little strange, they now willingly tell all. This is my fifth book about our much haunted country, and wherever possible I like to visit the places concerned and talk to those involved. Ghost stories are always interesting, but a good eye witness account is best of all.

Suffolk has some of the best stories I've encountered. I hope you will enjoy reading about them.

Betty Puttick

1

What's in a Name?

WHAT could bring a witch back some 350 years after death to make a nuisance of herself in a busy shop in the heart of Ipswich? In life this lady appears to have been a malevolent character who would have had no time at all for throwing flowers around and giving young assistants a playful push. Has time mellowed her, or has a most extraordinary coincidence had something to do with the return of someone whose last appearance in Ipswich was in 1645 when she met an horrific death by burning for the crime of petty treason?

In the spring of 1997 an interesting story appeared in the local *Star* newspaper regarding spooky goings-on at the Lakeland shop in the Butter Market. The well-known kitchen goods firm had only occupied Ipswich's historic Ancient House for a short time when they noticed odd things happening which were difficult to explain.

There had been special displays of flowers for Valentine's Day and again for Mothering Sunday, and overnight the staff found bunches had been moved and rearranged on the front door mat! And on another occasion when staff had taken flowers from their vases to another location, next day they found the flowers had somehow migrated back to their original places.

Sensibly they dismissed it as just one of those things, but other happenings aroused more apprehension. One member of staff had gone down to the cellar one day, but when she wanted to come back up she couldn't open the door. 'She had to force her way out,' said the Manager, 'but it's odd because there is absolutely no problem with the door and it never gets stuck.'

Another assistant said, 'I was getting my things together after work ready to go home, and I put my parking ticket on the side in the toilet. When I came back for it, the ticket had vanished. All the staff helped me look for it and we went over everywhere in the toilet and outside the door but couldn't find it. It caused me a lot of problems because I had to prove who I was when I went to get the car.

'Then the next morning the ticket was sitting at the opposite end of the toilet next to the skirting board. I couldn't believe it!'

Curiouser and curiouser! As the staff stacked the shelves, goods would fall off again of their own accord. In fact, one day when the sales team leader was walking past a window, a vase was suddenly swept off the windowsill in front of her. Instinctively she caught it, but it was a near thing! 'The window was open, but it wasn't a windy day,' she said. 'It was strange!'

Bottles of Coke vanished and reappeared in the fridge. And the incident of a locked cabinet was even stranger. The key had been mislaid, but although the cabinet couldn't be opened, the items on the shelves were seen to have been moved around leaving marks in the dust!

When I called at the shop in September 1997, one of the sales assistants told me that one day she had been down in the cellar when she felt someone pluck at her sleeve. Thinking it was another assistant she said, 'Just a minute, can't you see I'm busy?'

Although she then discovered that she was alone in the cellar, it didn't at first occur to her to think it might have been the ghost. 'But when I got back upstairs I realised,' she said, 'and I went cold all over!'

Nevertheless, she said that in spite of all the odd happenings, including unexplained footsteps, she felt that their unseen ghost was just mischievous, and not malevolent in any way.

The Manager decided to enlist the services of a medium who confirmed that the shop was definitely haunted by a female presence. She was getting the name 'Lakeland' she said, but since that was the name of the shop, it seemed hardly significant. But the *Star* reporter who covered the story pointed out that the name of a witch who was burned to death in Ipswich in September 1645 was Mary Lakeland! The coincidence seems almost incredible and I visited the Record Office to find out more about her.

A pamphlet including the confession of Mother Lakeland revealed surprisingly that she had been a 'Professour of Religion' for many years, 'and yet a witch (as she confessed) for the space of near twenty years.'

Her covenant with the Devil who gave her three imps, two little dogs and a mole, is described and her subsequent bewitching of her husband, who then died in great misery. His death was followed by those of a Mr Lawrence and his child whose lives were also 'taken away' because Mr Lawrence asked Mrs Lakeland for 12 shillings she owed him. An unfortunate maid also came to grief because she asked for the return of a shilling she had lent to the accused.

The pamphlet then goes on to describe the fate of Mr Beale, 'who had formerly been a suitor to her grandchild, and because he would not have her, she (Lakeland) burned a new ship that he was to go Master of, and sent also to torment him and take away his life.' All these crimes were said to have been achieved with the aid of her imps.

However, this time, although Mr Beale was said to be in a terrible physical condition, he survived to outlive Mother

Lakeland, and after her death his body began to heal rapidly.

In Richard Deacon's book *Matthew Hopkins, Witchfinder General* he quotes from the depositions relating to her trial, which describe Mr Beale as the 'tutor' of her grandchild, rather than the 'suitor' as he appears in the above confession. But whichever he was, although his condition was described by surgeons in evidence as 'consumed and rotting', unlike Mother Lakeland's other victims, he lived to see his tormentor perish.

When Mary Lakeland was tried at the Ipswich Summer Assizes, the infamous Witchfinder General, Matthew Hopkins, his side-kick John Stearne and 'searcher' Mary Phillips were ranging through East Anglia on their relentless vendetta against witches and it seems likely that Mary Lakeland was one of his victims.

A great many women who were convicted of witchcraft were hanged, so why was Mary Lakeland burnt at the stake? Despite many charges of witchcraft brought against her, her main crime was petty treason, that is the murder of her husband, for which the penalty was to be burnt to death.

In search of a connection between the Ancient House and Mary Lakeland, I contacted Pete Jennings, author of the booklet *Supernatural Ipswich*, who conducts the popular Gemini Ghost Tours, and he was able to provide the missing clue. Mary Lakeland's husband John was a barber of St Stephen's, Ipswich, and they must have been near neighbours of the Ancient House which stands on a corner formed by St Stephens Lane and the Butter Market. But despite the interesting coincidence of the name Lakeland, can we necessarily assume that she is the supernatural presence in the Ancient House, considering its long history?

The house was built in 1567 by a prosperous merchant on the very ground where he had his fish stall in earlier days. The site was then in the heart of the Fish Market, but when in 1601 the property passed into the hands of William Sparrowe, a man of influence in the town, the proximity of the Fish Market was not to his taste and he had it moved elsewhere.

At the time of the Civil War Puritan influence was strong in Ipswich, but the Sparrowe family were Royalist supporters. There is a tradition that Charles II was hidden in the Ancient House after the Battle of Worcester in 1651, and a sealed off secret room was discovered in 1801 which could have been his hiding place. After the Restoration the Ancient House became a splendid building, beautifully decorated with elaborate pargeting and the Royal coat of arms of Charles II.

In the *Tendring Witchcraft Revelations* it is hinted that a few of those condemned and executed as witches were Royalist agents uncovered by Parliamentarian Hopkins' network of informers. In his *Supernatural Ipswich*, Pete Jennings queries the possibility that Mary Lakeland could have been a Royalist informer tried on trumped up charges of witchcraft. Her fate by burning, however, was not because she was condemned as a witch, but because she was responsible for the death of her husband.

For many years the Ancient House was a bookshop, and Pete Jennings says that, while he was still at school, a girl he knew worked there as a Saturday girl and told him that the staff had been trying to scare her with stories of a ghostly lady!

He also says that St Stephens Lane has other ghosts! The disused church is now a Tourist Information Office where two spectral lady organists sometimes appear to the staff in the late afternoon. It is believed that they might be two sisters who tried to keep the church going and were bitterly disappointed when it was declared redundant.

No one has suggested that these ladies may sometimes stray down to the Ancient House to create a little mischief and mayhem. Somehow I think the favourite candidate responsible for the haunting of the Lakeland shop has to be Mary Lakeland. With such an intriguing coincidence, who could wish to doubt it?

2

The Ghost with the Christmas Post

CHRISTMAS is traditionally a time for ghost stories, the creepier the better, especially if they are told round a good roaring fire with a glass or two of mulled wine to chase away the shivers.

But Christmas is also a time when many of us are out and about after dark in wintry weather and the last thing we want to add to the hazards of icy roads is an eerie experience of a supernatural kind like this happening reported in the *Lowestoft Journal*.

One night around Christmas 1980 policeman Frank Colby and his wife Winifred were driving southwards to Lowestoft on the A12. They were a little way past the Hopton turn-off when Mr Colby had to brake sharply at the sight of an elderly figure slowly crossing the dual carriageway in front of his car.

It appeared to be an old man of rather strange appearance. In the car headlights the figure looked greyish white, almost misty, thickset and shortish, about 5′ 6″ tall, wearing a long shapeless coat which reached almost to his ankles, the collar hunched up round his neck. He seemed to be hatless with very spiky hair, and there was one other thing which caught observant Mr Colby's eye.

'I know it sounds daft,' he said later, 'but he had fantastically huge footwear. His boots were very big and he was lifting them well up as he plodded across.'

There was something else decidedly strange too. . .

'Suddenly I realised I could see right through him. The broken white line on the road was quite visible. It ran right up to him and I could see it continuing through him. That was a staggering shock.'

The figure reached the central reservation and disappeared! Mr Colby got out of his car and examined the grass verge but there was absolutely nowhere the figure could have gone.

Mr Colby's police work made him used to taking careful note of exactly what he saw and he made a rough sketch of the odd figure on the spot. And later when he made some enquiries he found that he was not alone in encountering what seemed to be a ghost on the stretch of the A12 running between Hopton and the junction known as Rackham's Corner.

The report which appeared in the *Lowestoft Journal* inspired accounts from a number of other people, including the recollection of an accident which had happened not long before Christmas twenty years earlier.

The daughter of Mr Ernest Tuttle said that as a child she used to travel with her father in his fish lorry, and he had often remarked how he disliked driving on the old Yarmouth road. Not long before he died he had seen a grey shadowy mist passing across the road, and couldn't tell just what it was.

Mr Tuttle travelled on that road nearly every day, and he always said that he felt that there was something strange about it. Pamela, his daughter, remembered him remarking, 'This is the piece of road I do not like.'

Then one night just before Christmas he was killed outright when his lorry hit a tree on the Yarmouth road on the northern side of Corton Long Lane. At the inquest it appeared that, although he was so familiar with the road, at a point where he should have turned a corner he had driven straight into the tree. There seemed to be no explanation for the accident and an open verdict was returned.

Several other motorists reported seeing a misty figure which disappeared in front of them on the same road, and a woman and her daughter driving from Lowestoft through Hopton in late 1978 thought they had run over a man in a raincoat who suddenly appeared in front of the car before they could stop. They got out and searched everywhere but there was no sign of a body.

In early November 1981, not long after Halloween, a young man called Andrew Cutajar was driving on the A12 from Lowestoft to Yarmouth on his way to play pool for his pub team. He had just reached Rackham's Corner when he noticed what he described as 'a grey misty hazy thing' ahead. At first he couldn't make out just what it was, but when he got closer he realised it was the figure of a man. Andrew, too, noticed a long cape or coat, hanging well below the man's knees, and big old-fashioned heavy boots. He also mentioned long straggly grey hair.

'I would put him at about 60,' he said. 'Everything about him seemed grey. He was standing about two feet into the slow lane, and showing no sign of moving. I was getting closer, and still he didn't move, so I slammed on the brakes. If it had been a dry night I would have had no trouble, but the road was wet and I skidded.

'I must have blinked for a second, expecting some sort of bang or crunch – I was heading straight for him. When I opened my eyes I saw the radiator grille going straight through him!'

Andrew drew up and, feeling distinctly shaken, got out,

not knowing what he would find. But there was absolutely nothing! The ghostly stranger had vanished!

Feeling unable to continue to his pools match, Andrew turned back for home. He hesitated to tell his friends about his unnerving experience in case they thought he was crazy, but his mother got in touch with the police and Andrew soon discovered that, like policeman Frank Colby, he was one of many who had encountered the phantom of the A12.

Mr Ivan Bunn, a local psychic investigator, tried to discover something to account for the haunting, and in December 1988 he told the *Lowestoft Journal* that there was a strong possibility that the strange figure could be the ghost of William Balls, a postman who died while faithfully delivering his letters in Hopton in January 1899.

William with his 30 to 40 lb sack of mail covered the area of Hopton, Corton, Blundeston and Lound twice a day, and just before Christmas he had not been well. His doctor advised him that he should take a break from work but William was determined to deliver the Christmas mail as usual. He took a couple of days' rest after that, but 2nd January 1899 found him back on the job. No doubt the winter weather was too much for him as he trudged along with his heavy postbag, and he must have collapsed as his body was found by the side of the road in Hopton.

So if one winter night around Christmastime you are driving along on the A12 near Hopton, keep a wary eye open for a shadowy figure crossing the road ahead. It could be William Balls, still determined to deliver his letters over a hundred years late!

3

The Rougham Mirage

STORIES of the supernatural are full of haunted houses and apparitions, but a house that is an apparition is not so common. Just when this phenomenon first made its appearance I do not know, but we have an excellent eye witness account dating back to a warm summer evening in 1860.

Mr Robert Palfrey was busy thatching a new haystack in a field in the Kingshall Street area between the villages of Rougham and Bradfield St George, just a few miles outside Bury St Edmunds. As he worked his attention was caught by a strange sound like a 'swoosh' of air, and when he looked round he couldn't believe his eyes. Where just before there had been a familiar empty field, now he was looking at a large red brick double-fronted house behind ornate iron gates. The flower beds were in full bloom in front of the prosperous well-kept residence which Mr Palfrey, a longtime resident in the area, had never seen before.

Feeling rather stunned by this extraordinary happening, Mr Palfrey climbed down his ladder to take a better look, but when he did there was now nothing to see. Just as suddenly as it had appeared, the house had completely vanished, and Mr Palfrey became aware of a noticeable change in the atmosphere. It had been a warm summer evening, but now there was an unseasonal chill in the air, and Mr Palfrey felt, too, a cold stab of fear as he realised that he had witnessed something decidedly uncanny.

When he arrived home, his wife and family could see that he was not his usual self, and when he told them what had happened they all decided to walk back to where he had been working to have another look. But, of course, the mysterious house did not give a repeat performance, and poor Mr Palfrey was the subject of a good deal of good-natured teasing.

But by an extraordinary coincidence, Mr Palfrey's great-grandson James Cobbold was to have much the same experience many years later. James's grandmother was Emily Cobbold, Mr Palfrey's daughter, who kept a little general shop in Beyton, and as a boy James used to help George Waylett, the butcher next door, on Saturdays when he went round in his pony cart delivering meat in the Rougham and Bradfield St George area.

It was James's job to look after the pony and one Saturday morning in June 1912 they were driving along Kingshall Street from Rougham, towards Bradfield St George. They were about three or four hundred yards from the T-junction where the road branches off towards Bradfield when there was a sudden 'swooshing' noise, and to their astonishment a double-fronted red brick house of Georgian style materialised on the side of the road near Colville Grove.

The sound startled the pony which reared up, pitching poor George Waylett off the back of the cart onto the road, leaving James hanging onto the reins for dear life trying to control the bolting horse. At last he managed to pull up, and turned back to help Mr Waylett. In spite of the sudden shock of it all, James had clearly registered not only the large three-storeyed house, but also the flower beds in front, all in full bloom with geraniums, pansies and standard rose trees. And he certainly noticed how cold it had become. It had been a hot, sunny June morning, but with the arrival of the house the temperature had turned icy cold!

But James could see that the house was gradually disappearing in a kind of mist as he reached Mr Waylett, who was picking himself up muttering, with a few choice swear words, 'That ———— house! That's about the third time I've seen that happen!'

In spite of feeling scared, James's curiosity made him scramble through the hedge into the field where the house had been only a few short minutes before. It was full of growing wheat and James fully expected to find the crop flattened, but there was nothing to show where the house had stood. The crop was waving gently in the summer breeze as if nothing had happened.

James Cobbold wrote the story for *Amateur Gardening* in December 1975, and again, under a pseudonym, for the *East Anglian Magazine* in February 1982 when he was 81. There were still people who heard the story with amused disbelief he said, but he had found several other eye witnesses of the curious Rougham mirage, and horses shied when passing the spot and dogs had been known to raise their hackles and bare their teeth for no apparent reason.

Another sighting is mentioned in John Harries' *Ghost Hunter's Road Book* published in 1968. In 1926 Miss Wynne, a local school teacher, and her teenage pupil Ruth Allison were walking one afternoon in the Kingshall Street area towards Bradfield St George church. Miss Wynne's father was the new Vicar at Rougham, so the district was quite unfamiliar to her at the time, and when they noticed a large double-fronted house partly hidden by trees, behind a wall and large wrought iron gates, they wondered who lived there.

When they made enquiries they were assured that there was no house of that description in the area. And shortly afterwards when they walked along the same route, they were amazed to find that there was no wall, no gates, and no house, just a ditch and a wilderness of weeds. Only the trees seemed to be the same.

When some time later an appeal was made on air for cases of ghostly apparitions, Miss Wynne described her experience and it was featured on BBC radio. She said, 'I have often been past the site since, but I have never seen it again. I am not what might be called psychic, and this is the only experience of the kind I have ever had.'

So did a house of the style described once stand on the side of Kingshall Street near the woodland known as Colville's Grove? Witnesses have all received local people's assurance that there never has been such a property there and, in any case, a substantial building of Georgian design would hardly have been demolished and forgotten by 1860 when Robert Palfrey saw the strange mirage.

The 'swooshing' sound as the house arrived suggests a displacement of air as if it was transported from elsewhere. One wonders what would happen if anyone were close enough to walk up to the house, or even enter it!

There are other examples when this seems to have actually happened! In the 1930s Edna Hedges, then a young girl, was cycling along Ermine Street, outside Swindon, when it started to rain heavily. Noticing a thatched cottage with smoke coming from the chimney she decided to ask for shelter, and an old gentleman let her into a low ceilinged room lit by a bright fire to take cover from the storm.

Then suddenly she found herself back on the road, although she had no recollection of leaving the cottage, and when she told friends what had happened, she was assured that there was no such cottage on that road, except an old derelict one, empty for many years. She went back herself later and found a ruined cottage in an overgrown garden. And yet she is quite sure that what she described really did happen. But thinking about it she realised that although there was quite a storm outside, there was no noise inside the cottage, and the old gentleman had simply stood there smiling, and said nothing.

In 1987 two members of the Lochaber mountain rescue team were at the summit of Ben Finlay, a Ross-shire peak, when they noticed a two-storey lodge on the shores of Loch Mullardoch about two miles away. They decided to shelter there for the night, and began the climb down with the lodge still in their view until a ridge obscured it. But when they reached the loch, the building had disappeared.

They told the Scottish *Sunday Mail* that they had both spotted the lodge independently of each other although it had not appeared on their map. But they later found that a shooting lodge in the same part of the valley vanished under water when a dam was built there over forty years before.

This report produced a letter from a man who said that in June 1951 he had demolished a lodge which he thinks must have been the one the climbers saw. This was done in case its chimneys became a danger to boats.

Another phantom cottage has been seen several times in a wood near Haytor, Devon. A newcomer to the area admired it as she walked by in the lane and mentioned it to the wood's owner, who was surprised as there was no cottage there. Soon after, someone else who had recently come to live nearby noticed the cottage, and also an Ordnance Surveyor, looking down from a height, saw a cottage and realised he must have missed it before. From above he could see smoke coming from the chimney and a line of washing blowing in the breeze. And yet when he reached the area there was no trace of it.

A woman walking home through the city streets of Michigan late one night in 1973 glanced up at the moon, and when she looked back her surroundings had completely changed. Just ahead was an old thatched cottage, and as she walked up to the gate she saw a man and woman in very old-fashioned clothes sitting in the garden, and a little dog ran towards her barking. The man looked up and called to the dog to be quiet, and the woman at the gate realised he didn't see her. Then as she glanced back the way she had come, there was her familiar street once more. Suddenly the cottage had vanished, and she found she was only a few yards from her own front door.

One could continue with similar experiences, but who can explain them? One of the most famous time-slips is the visit of Miss Jourdain and Miss Moberley to Versailles in August 1901, when they apparently walked into the gardens of the Petit Trianon as they were in the 1770s. They met and spoke to people dressed in the costume of the time of Marie Antoinette, in fact they saw a woman sitting painting whom they believed to have been the Queen herself. They described a feeling of oppressive dreaminess, 'as if', one said, 'I was walking in my sleep.'

More recently, on 1st May 1996 the *Daily Mail* reported that when a man living in an apartment block in Limehouse, East London looked at the view from his video entry phone at night, he saw a terrace of Victorian houses. But what he should have seen is the apartment block opposite, which he does see quite normally by day.

He wondered if the Victorian houses had originally stood where the apartment block is now, but on enquiry he found that an old biscuit factory had previously occupied the site.

What is really odd is that when visitors arrive, and he looks at his video entry phone, he sees them superimposed in front of the Victorian houses! As he says, there really is no logical explanation for it. Or indeed for any of the other phantom buildings that appear like a paranormal conjuring trick, only to vanish as if by magic.

Perhaps one day soon someone else walking along Kingshall Street between Rougham and Bradfield St George will hear a 'swoosh', and there in the field will be that double-fronted house of Georgian style with the pretty garden. Or perhaps you have already seen it? It would be nice to know.

4

A Dream of Murder

THE small Suffolk village of Polstead is famous for two things, a cherry with a unique flavour that they grow there called the Polstead Black, and a murder that has never been forgotten. Fascination with the crime may have been due to the unusual dramatic circumstance that the body was discovered through a dream, or because the re-enactment of the *Murder in the Red Barn* became one of the most popular melodramas ever staged.

Hastily written versions featuring the innocent young village maiden and the wicked squire were filling provincial theatres and fairground booths almost immediately after the trial, and the play has continued to be performed somewhere ever since, with a film in 1935, and a television drama in 1980.

Maria Marten, the village molecatcher's pretty daughter, was the local femme fatale, and Thomas Corder, the eldest son of a wealthy farmer, became her lover. But Maria's hopes of a better position in life were dashed when she became pregnant and Thomas would have no more to do with her.

The baby did not survive, and Maria soon found another well-to-do admirer, Peter Matthews, who introduced her to the high life in London. Yet again, Maria became pregnant but when her son, Thomas Henry, was born, Matthews proved more honourable than her previous lover, and gave her a regular allowance which was very welcome at the cottage where her father lived with his young second wife and family. Still flighty and irresponsible, Maria often left her child to be cared for by Anne, her stepmother, while she enjoyed life in the nearby towns with various admirers. But during a visit home in the spring of 1826 she met her fate in the shape of William Corder, Thomas Corder's younger brother.

William was only about 5' 4" tall, with a slight stoop, freckles and large turned up nose, and although he was intelligent with ambitions to become a writer or a teacher, his father insisted that he should work on the family farm. Discontented with his life he took to drinking and bad company, so his father sent him to join the Merchant Navy. But, rejected through poor eyesight, he stayed on in London gambling and drinking until his money ran out. Then soon after his return to Polstead his father died suddenly in 1825, leaving Thomas and William to run the farm.

On a spring day in 1826 Maria was working in the garden when William passed by the Martens' cottage, and her smile captivated him. They began seeing each other, although William was anxious to keep their relationship secret from his family. The old red barn which belonged to the Corders seemed an ideal place to meet, out of sight of the village gossips, but inevitably, with her unfortunate record, Maria was soon pregnant. Unlike his brother Thomas, William did not walk out on her, in fact he told her father and stepmother that he would marry Maria as soon as he could.

But there was even more trouble in store when in February 1827 Thomas Corder was accidentally drowned in the village pond leaving William now the mainstay of the Corder family, as his two younger brothers both suffered from tuberculosis.

With the birth of Maria's baby approaching, William

31

was desperate to spare his mother this added distress, so Maria went to Sudbury where her child was born on 16th April. But soon after she returned home her ailing baby died, and was secretly buried by Corder and Maria.

Despite the Marten family's hopes that Corder would soon marry Maria, his arrival on Friday, 18th May, insisting that they set off at once for Ipswich to be married, was a complete surprise. Still anxious to keep his plans secret from his family he told Maria to disguise herself in men's clothing while he took a bag with her best clothes to the Red Barn. While he was gone Maria reluctantly put on a man's suit, but apparently insisted on wearing her own underwear and petticoat underneath. She crammed a man's hat on top of her upswept hair, and when Corder returned, they left the Martens' cottage by different doors, and went over the fields to the barn.

Not surprisingly, Anne Marten, Maria's stepmother, had misgivings as she saw them go. Corder's behaviour seemed strange, and Maria was tearful about all the rush and secrecy. It was to be the last time Anne would see Maria alive.

A few days later Mrs Marten was amazed to see Corder back in Polstead, and he gave her a garbled explanation about the licence having to be signed in London before they could be married. Maria was staying with friends, he said, and over the next few months Corder constantly assured her all was well, giving a variety of reasons why Maria didn't write home.

But Anne Marten still felt uneasy. Then on 18th October the Martens received a letter from Corder saying that he and Maria were married, and asking if they had received Maria's letter telling them all about the happy day. No such letter had arrived and Corder's request that the

Martens should burn all letters so that no one could discover their address was not reassuring.

Meanwhile in London, Corder had placed advertisements in newspapers seeking 'an agreeable lady desirous of meeting a tender, kind and sympathising companion'! He collected 45 replies, and a further 54 arrived later, which Corder never returned to collect.

Corder obviously planned to start a new life, and Mary Moore, one of his correspondents, seemed an ideal partner. She was a pretty and accomplished young teacher, and they were married by special licence in December and straightaway set up a small boarding school in Brentford together.

But Corder could not shake off the past and suffered restless nights haunted by bad dreams. Anne Marten back in Polstead was also a prey to nightmares and often disturbed her husband by crying out as she tossed and turned. She felt that Maria was calling out to her for help and for three nights running she dreamed that Maria was murdered and buried in the Red Barn. In the end her husband was forced to take her seriously.

So on the 19th April Thomas Marten reluctantly agreed to visit the Red Barn with an old friend who worked for the Corders and make a search of the bay in the right-hand corner as his wife wanted.

And there, just as Anne had seen in her dream, Thomas found the body of his daughter in a shallow grave. At first he could not identify her until he noticed a goitre on the neck which Maria had and, although Anne could not bear to visit the barn, when she saw some of the clothing from the body she recognised items Maria had worn on the day she left with Corder.

Corder was soon traced by police, and Maria's reticule and a pair of Corder's pistols were found at the house. He was arrested and came for trial on 7th August before a packed courtroom at Bury St Edmunds, charged with mortally wounding Maria with a pistol shot, stabbing with a sharp instrument, wounding with a sword, strangling with a handkerchief and suffocating with earth, to all of which he replied 'Not Guilty'.

There were many witnesses, Anne Marten's testimony being the most dramatic. Various experts thought that the pistol shot to the head alone could not have killed Maria, and great consternation was caused in court when a surgeon actually produced her head to illustrate the direction of the bullet!

Corder spoke at length in his own defence. He said he and Maria quarrelled when they reached the Red Barn and, angered by her attitude, he walked out. But as he went away he heard a shot and went back to find Maria had shot herself with one of his pistols and was dead. He realised how bad the situation would look for himself and in a panic he buried the body. He suggested that the stab wounds on the body had been caused by her father's mole spade when he discovered the grave.

But after only 35 minutes the jury returned a verdict of Guilty and he was sentenced to hang. While he was in prison, the prison Governor and the Chaplain urged Corder to confess so that he could die with a clear conscience, and he finally admitted his guilt. A copy of the confession was then immediately rushed out to waiting pressmen, and by the time Corder mounted the scaffold copies were already on sale in London, Sudbury and Bury St Edmunds.

The execution was timed for 12 noon on 11th August 1828 and crowds assembled at Bury Jail from early morning, reaching many thousands by the time William Corder was launched into eternity. The body was rushed to the Shire Hall for the crowds to file past, and the hangman sold pieces of the rope for a guinea an inch. Next day the body was removed to the County Hospital for dissection by the County Surgeon, George Creed, who later tanned some of the skin and used it to bind a book about the murder and trial which is now in Moyses Hall Museum in Bury.

Even more macabre, by 1841 Corder's skeleton had been installed in a glass case in the West Suffolk Hospital where, as visitors approached, a spring caused the arm to point to a charity box below! Later the skeleton, known to the nurses as George, was used for anatomy classes.

When I visited the ancient building that houses Moyses Hall Museum I found a glass case with relics of the Red Barn murder. There is the book mentioned above, a bust of Corder used in the 'newly fashionable Phrenology', a repulsive object said to be Corder's scalp, also tanned by George Creed, two of Corder's pistols and one of the souvenirs sold at the time, a snuff box made from a piece of the Red Barn. Copies of some of the catchpenny broadsheets also on sale at the time are available at the Museum, but my attention was caught by a full size photograph of Corder's skeleton on the wall by the case of relics. There was something odd about the skull I thought. Corder was only a young man, about 25 at the time of his death, and yet the skull, particularly the crooked, worn old teeth, appeared to belong to someone much older. However, before long I came across an explanation for that as you will see from the next chapter.

Maria's body was buried in the local churchyard but today there is just a wooden board on a small outbuilding to say that her grave is nearby. Her gravestone was gradually chipped away by ghoulish souvenir hunters until nothing remains.

The grim melodrama of the Red Barn murder was soon being played out on many a stage. The best known portrayal came from Tod Slaughter, an actor famous for his bloodcurdling roles as Sweeney Todd the Demon Barber, Jekyll and Hyde, and Jack the Ripper. He was a huge man with a voice to match, and anyone less like William Corder would be hard to imagine. Strangely enough, his role in the Red Barn play was his last. He died in his sleep in February 1956 after being hanged on stage in his role as Corder! It was said he had murdered Maria Marten on stage at least 2,000 times!

Some plays featured Maria's ghost making a dramatic appearance in the condemned cell, but apart from the supernatural element of Anne Marten's dreams which led to the discovery of the murder, there seem to have been no sightings of poor Maria since her death. There are stories of a shadowy figure in an old-fashioned frock coat and hat, resembling Corder, gliding through the garden of the old timber-framed gabled house at the foot of the hill in Polstead where Corder once lived. It has been seen several times on the anniversary of the murder, moving away from the house in the direction of the Martens' cottage in Martens Lane.

But there is a much more chilling ghost story concerning Corder which deserves a chapter of its own. Read on...

5

The Strange Story of Corder's Skull

WHEN the author and ghost hunter R. Thurston Hopkins was young he lived in Gyves House, within the walls of the old prison at Bury St Edmunds. His father was an official in the Prison Service, and Hopkins recalled that at his home there was a framed letter, the last confession of William Corder, hanged on 11th August 1828 for the murder of Maria Marten.

Hopkins' father had a close friend, Dr Kilner, a Bury doctor with a rather macabre interest in the Red Barn murder, in fact the former surgeon at Bury Jail who bound a book about the murder in Corder's skin and also pickled Corder's scalp, bequeathed these grisly relics to Dr Kilner in his will.

But Dr Kilner also had a fancy to own Corder's skull which had been at the West Suffolk General Hospital for some fifty years, as part of the skeleton which was used for anatomy lessons. But how to acquire it? Dr Kilner, a well respected medical practitioner, decided there was nothing for it but a little midnight sleight of hand!

Hopkins' father, who later became involved, thoroughly enjoyed regaling family and guests at Christmastime with the macabre story of what happened next, every word of which he swore was absolutely true.

When Dr Kilner arrived at the hospital museum in the

middle of the night to perform his skulduggery, he lit three candles. It was odd that one candle immediately went out, and as he relit it, the flames of the other two also vanished. As he removed the skull from Corder's skeleton, the candles kept up the same irritating behaviour as first one and then another went out as if they were snuffed by an invisible hand. But Dr Kilner was not put off, as soon as he had Corder's skull he wired another spare anatomical skull in its place and made his escape before he was discovered!

He had his prize polished, mounted and installed in a square ebony box which he placed in a cabinet in his drawing room, but as he confided to Hopkins Senior, from the moment the skull was in his possession he felt uneasy about it. He was not the kind of man to imagine that the skull could be haunted. All that kind of thing was mumbo-jumbo in his opinion, and surely after so many years at the hospital being used by doctors and students, any supernatural influence must have disappeared long since.

A few days after the skull was installed at Dr Kilner's home his servant came to tell him that a gentleman had called to see him. The doctor was not pleased as it was after surgery hours, and when he asked her if the caller was a patient she recognised, she replied that she had never seen him before. 'He is proper old-fashioned looking,' she said, 'with a furry top hat and a blue overcoat with silver buttons.'

The doctor went to the surgery to see his visitor, asking the servant to bring a lamp as it was getting dark. As he looked into the room, he had the impression that there was someone standing by the window, but when the servant followed him in with the lamp, there was no one there.

The servant insisted that a gentleman had called and been shown into the surgery, but it looked as if he must have changed his mind and decided not to wait.

The doctor thought little of the incident, but one evening soon afterwards he was looking out of the window when he noticed a figure at the end of the lawn by the summer-house. Someone who was wearing a beaver hat and an old-fashioned great coat! The doctor stepped out into the garden to accost the intruder, but before he could reach him, the figure vanished.

Dr Kilner found these two incidents disturbing, and during subsequent days he often had the uneasy sensation that someone was following him. At night he sometimes heard doors opening and the sound of footsteps passing through the house. Even worse was the heavy breathing and muttering outside bedroom doors, and sometimes the sound of hammering and sobbing coming from the drawing room below. And in his restless sleep there were dreams in which someone seemed to be pleading with him. In the end sleep became impossible and despite his usual dismissive and robust attitude to the supernatural, the doctor had no doubt that it was the skull in his drawing room that was the cause of what was happening.

It seemed obvious that the ghost of William Corder wanted his skull and skeleton to be reunited, but this was impossible. Now that the skull had been polished, the difference would immediately be noticed if he put it back. And he would have to admit that he, a respectable doctor, had taken it! It was a dreadful dilemma. One night he had scarcely fallen asleep before something woke him. It was a sound downstairs, and he listened for a moment or two before lighting a candle and quietly walking out onto the landing. Looking down over the stair-rail he could just see the glass handle of the drawing room door and as he looked a hand closed over it, although he could not see anyone, simply a disembodied hand. Then as he watched the door knob was slowly turned and quietly the door of the drawing room opened.

The doctor had been so absorbed in what was happening that he was almost startled out of his wits by what occurred next. There was a loud explosion, almost as if someone had fired a gun in the drawing room, and pausing only to grasp a heavy candlestick as a weapon, the doctor ran downstairs to the drawing room. But as he reached the door a tremendous gust of wind met him, blowing out his candle and enveloping him in what seemed like a malevolent force. He felt as if he was fighting his way into the room, where he struggled to strike a match to relight his candle.

Then as the light flickered over the room he saw that the box which held Corder's skull was shattered into minute fragments. The door to the cabinet where the box had been was open, and on the shelf stood the skull, grinning evilly.

Dr Kilner could not wait to get rid of it. In view of their friendship, it seems rather strange that he offered the skull to Hopkins Senior, who walked home with it wrapped in a silk handkerchief. On his way he twisted his foot and fell heavily on the steps of the Angel Hotel, just as a lady of his acquaintance was passing. As the skull rolled at her feet she screamed, staring at it in horror, then hurried by without a word. There was nothing that Hopkins Senior could say in explanation, and apparently the lady in question never referred to it afterwards.

The twisted foot kept Mr Hopkins in bed for a week, and shortly afterwards his best mare rolled into a chalk pit and broke her back. Illness, sorrow and financial disaster followed for both Hopkins and Kilner, leaving them almost bankrupt, and it was obvious that the skull's reign of terror had to be broken. Mr Hopkins' solution was to take it to a country churchyard not far from Bury St Edmunds and bribe a gravedigger to give it a Christian burial.

To everyone's relief this apparently broke the spell, and in due course peace and good fortune returned.

'You will say that this story is an invention,' wrote R. Thurston Hopkins in his book *Ghosts Over England* published in 1953. 'But you will be greatly mistaken. Names, places and events are openly and correctly stated, and can be verified. So if ever you come across a tortoise-shell-tinted skull in a japanned cash box, leave it severely alone. If you take it home there will be the Devil to Pay – and you may not be prepared to meet his bill!'

6

Ghosts of the Highways and Byways

IN the spring of 1970 a Lowestoft man was driving home in the early hours on the Beccles-Lowestoft road. He was on the Beccles side of Barnby when he had to brake hard to avoid a cyclist wheeling his bicycle along in the middle of the road.

The man's appearance was so sudden that the driver, Alan Stevens, nearly put his head through the windscreen as he jammed on his brakes but before his car came to a halt the cyclist had disappeared.

'He seemed to be dressed in black knee-length breeches with white stockings. I saw a white mudguard and a red reflector,' said Mr Stevens afterwards. The man had been right in front of his car, and yet in a split second he was gone.

'I don't know whether I believe or disbelieve in ghosts, but I certainly saw this one,' said Mr Stevens, who mentioned the incident to several friends afterwards and found that other people had had a similar experience on the Beccles to Lowestoft road.

When a report appeared in the local press, Mr B.H. Davy of Yarmouth suggested that the ghost may have been his father Frederick, who used to have a watchmaker and jeweller's business in Yarmouth, and who was killed while cycling midway between Blind Man's Gate and Barnby church in April 1916. 'He was in the middle of the road like the apparition and he was wearing the same kind of breeches,' said his son. 'The only thing is that he was killed on the opposite side of Barnby from where the ghost was seen.

'There is another strange thing about this. My father was 54 when he was killed and that was 54 years ago this month.'

Another phantom cyclist used to frequent the road between the Sedge Inn at Lakenheath and Farthing Drove, known to local people as Old Sillitoe or 'Steeltoes'. Eye witnesses reported that the bicycle glowed eerily with a greenish light, just bright enough to show the outline of Old Sillitoe as he pedalled along where the road runs for a mile or so beside a ditch.

This ghost had a sinister reputation, and people who happened to be in the area around midnight kept a wary eye open as the phantom cyclist had been known to buffet any traveller who was in his way. In fact in 1950 the body of a young Irish labourer was discovered in the ditch, his bicycle lying overturned on the road. He had left the nearby inn a little the worse for drink at closing time and could possibly have lost his balance and pitched over into the ditch. Or did he encounter the menacing phantom cyclist with dire results? It's said that later an exorcism was conducted in the area frequented by Old Sillitoe which seems to have proved effective.

A much more ancient form of transport haunts the Beccles area. Phantom coaches driven by headless coachmen are a popular feature of ghostlore, and tradition says that Roos Hall, Beccles, on the Lowestoft to Bungay road, receives a far more gruesome visitor than Santa

Claus on Christmas Eve. Out of the mists of Barsham Marshes emerges a ghostly coach and four driven by the regulation headless coachman and sweeps up to the front door of the Hall.

The huge oak which stands in the grounds of Roos Hall was once the town gibbet, and locals say that if you walk six times round it the Devil will appear. There is also another apparition said to haunt the Hall's guest room, where inside the wardrobe can be seen the Devil's footprint on the wall!

The Walberswick and Blythburgh area has ghost stories galore, and just before Christmas 1977 a long distance lorry driver had an unexpected close encounter which left him considerably shaken.

He was driving along the A12 at Blythburgh Common where the road undulates up and down a series of small hills, and as he came up a rise he was forced to skid to a stop as he saw right in front of him a large black horse. Walking beside the horse and holding the reins was a man in knee breeches and what the driver described as a Dick Turpin coat and hat, like a highwayman, and holding his arm was a young girl in a long dress and poke bonnet.

The driver jumped out of his lorry, afraid that he might have hit the horse, but to his amazement, when he hurried round to the front of his vehicle the road was quite empty and the unusual trio had vanished. At first glance he had taken them to be real, but now it seemed all too likely that he had seen ghosts.

He arrived at a guest house in Kessingland where he usually stayed, very shaken by his experience. The landlady described him as a steady chap who had not been drinking and certainly was not the sort to imagine things, but as he said, 'I never believed in ghosts, but I do now.'

At the time the lorry driver thought that his curious experience was a unique happening. But there is a history of previous sightings in the same area of a man and girl with a horse dating back more than two hundred years, and the clothes worn suggest a period during the 18th century.

The local explanation for the haunting relates to a farmer or farm labourer who worked in the Blythburgh Common area. He had a niece who used to bring his lunch each day, but one day he dropped dead while ploughing and she found him lying on the ground beside his horse.

It is difficult to imagine why many years afterwards a spectral re-enactment of a journey this trio may often have taken should be seen by someone with no previous psychic experience. It would be interesting to know whether previous sightings have been at the same time of year.

7

The Return of Henrietta

WHEN collector Bryan Hall was the victim of an armed robbery at his home in 1995, he warned the thieves that they may have acquired something unexpected as well as the stolen antiques – a ghost! For one of the paintings they stole, a portrait by East Anglian artist William Johnson, is haunted!

'The thieves made a big mistake in stealing Henrietta, for her restless spirit won't do them any good,' said Mr Hall. 'Her ghost follows the portrait wherever it goes, and over the years many people have experienced unusual occurrences caused by the lady in the wide-brimmed hat.'

The painting of Henrietta Nelson, a pale, unsmiling lady in a huge beribbonned hat, had been in Mr Hall's possession for nearly 50 years, but he has known the strange story of this unusual portrait since his youth. Miss Nelson died at Yaxley Hall in Suffolk in April 1816 at the age of 82 after falling down a short flight of stairs from her bedroom, and according to tradition she had a strong objection to being buried in the family vault. So in keeping with her wishes a handsome mausoleum was built in the Hall grounds near the path to the church, and here she rested in peace until some years later when a new owner decided to demolish Henrietta's mausoleum and remove her to the family vault.

After that her restless spirit took to wandering around the garden and grounds and was seen by the family at the Hall and their servants, and it was noticed that her portrait had a startling ability to change expression. The Rev Edmund Farrer who once owned the portrait commented that, not surprisingly, this had a disturbing effect upon the minds of his friends. Joan Forman, too, described in her *Haunted East Anglia* that when she visited Mr Hall and first saw the portrait, she felt quite uncomfortable under Miss Nelson's disapproving and hostile gaze. However, she made some sympathetic comment and was amazed, on taking a last look at the picture before she left, to find that Henrietta's expression now appeared quite amiable!

'As a portrait it was fascinating, the face was very much alive,' Mr Hall told me, adding that now it had gone the house seemed absolutely empty. He felt sure that her spirit had left with the picture.

Henrietta Nelson lived at Yaxley Hall with the Leeke family. Madame Margaret Seymour, who bought the Hall in 1736, is delicately described in the Rev Edmund Farrer's history of Yaxley Hall as the favourite lady of Nicholas, 4th Earl of Scarsdale, by whom she had three children, Nicholas, Seymour and Margaret.

The Rev Farrer passes on the interesting tit-bit that at the time of his death in 1736 the Earl had eighty living children but Madame Seymour's offspring were the only ones allowed to bear his family name of Leeke. Madame Seymour died in 1740 leaving Yaxley to her elder son, Nicholas, and other possessions and jewellery 'to be equally divided between my three children'. There was no mention of Henrietta, although it was suspected that Madame Seymour was her mother through an illicit liaison with an estate worker.

Henrietta was said to have been treated as an inferior by the family because of the stigma of her illegitimacy. The unfairness of this must have been hard to bear as although illegitimate themselves they presumably considered that bearing the Earl's name gave them superiority. Certainly her objection to sharing the family tomb with Madame Seymour suggests that Henrietta cherished a deep resentment to the end of her days.

However, Henrietta continued to live as part of the family at Yaxley Hall and when it passed to Nicholas's son Francis in 1786 the Rev Farrer describes the subsequent thirty years together as 'a long spell of domestic felicity'. From diaries and account books Mr Farrer gathered that life at Yaxley Hall was a lively social round of visitors, dinner parties, theatre visits, with yearly trips to London and elsewhere. Apparently both Francis and Henrietta liked riding, and the purchase of an 'extravagant' bridle costing £2 7s 0d is recorded for Mrs Nelson!

So presumably life looked up considerably for Henrietta during her later years, but her final wishes about the mausoleum suggest that the hurt feelings had not been forgotten.

Eventually it became apparent that wherever Henrietta's portrait went her ghost would follow. When it went to a house at Barton Turf, a ghostly face, recognisably Henrietta, was seen looking out of a bedroom window. And later when the painting was moved to Smallburgh, she was seen again, looking through a kitchen window. She was dressed as she was in her portrait, but her face and clothing were the colour of parchment. And subsequently when the portrait came into Mr Hall's possession, there were reported sightings of Henrietta's ghost walking in the grounds of his home.

In the early 1950s there was an auction which included

property from Yaxley Hall, and when Bryan Hall arrived at the marquee where it was being held the first thing he saw was Miss Nelson's portrait propped up, staring at him!

'I bought it for £15,' he told me.

He added that when reports of the armed robbery in 1995 appeared in the press, someone who had lived in Yaxley Hall in the 1940s telephoned him. She said that while doing restoration work she and her husband had noticed some loose plaster, and behind it they found a doll! It had both legs broken and was dressed to resemble Miss Nelson as she appeared in her portrait.

Even more curious, they found that if they left the doll in the window on the right of the front door, next morning when they went downstairs they would find the doll on the left by the fireplace!

So where is the portrait now, and has the ghost of Henrietta Nelson followed her custom and accompanied it? Possibly it has been sold to someone unaware of its strange history. It seems unlikely that we have heard the last of Miss Henrietta Nelson.

8

The Haunt of the Black Dog

MOST areas have their own particular ghosts but there is one supernatural creature that knows no boundaries. The terror of the Black Dog spreads like a stain over much of the country although each area has its own name for the huge beast with glowing eyes which pads silently along lonely lanes, ancient tracks and coastal paths. Alarming as his appearance may be to a lone traveller, tradition has it that a sighting is also an omen of death and disaster to the terrified onlooker. But the number of witnesses who have encountered the devil dog and lived to tell the tale give the lie to this superstition.

In the North of England he is the Padfoot, Shriker or Trash, in Norfolk Black Shuck or the Snarleyow, and in Suffolk he is Shuck or the Galleytrot, whereas in Wales there is a whole pack of devil dogs, the Cwm Annum, the creatures of Annwn, King of the Underworld, said to be the souls of those doomed to wander for ever in purgatory. Seen alone there, he is the Gwyllgi, known as the dog of darkness.

Dartmoor, too, has its legendary pack of hellhounds which range that bleak wilderness, but it is believed to be during a holiday in Cromer that Conan Doyle got the inspiration for his Hound of the Baskervilles, when he first heard about Black Shuck.

East Anglia has many tales of the Black Dog and on stormy nights tough old fishermen would say that this is the kind of weather when he is likely to be abroad, his blood-chilling howl rising above the sound of the wind.

The Galleytrot is reputed to have been seen near Leiston church, in the large churchyard fringed by lime trees and filled with ancient gravestones green with lichen. But when I was there no black hound made an appearance, not even a friendly labrador.

In the early 1900s, two aristocratic ladies, Lady Walsingham and Lady Rendlesham, once sat up one night in the churchyard hoping for a glimpse of the legendary hound. Sure enough, at midnight, they saw slinking between the gravestones a dark shadowy form which leapt over the churchyard wall and disappeared down the lane.

Ancient tracks are haunts of the Black Dog, and he is said to range along the Devil's Ditch, a defensive earthwork which peters out close to the village of Reach, just over the border in Cambridgeshire. It runs as far as Newmarket Heath, crossing the A11 and A14 north of the roundabout where the roads join.

In his *Ghost Book*, Alasdair Alpin MacGregor reports that one evening in the early autumn of 1938 an Aldeburgh man was on his way home from Bungay, walking towards Ditchingham station. He noticed a black object approaching, and as it got nearer he could see that it was a large black dog with a long shaggy coat. It was on the same side of the road and he moved into the centre of the road to let it pass, but as it drew level with him, it vanished! Naturally he recounted this extraordinary experience to his friends in the 'local', and was told that Black Shuck was known to frequent the neighbourhood and quite a number of people had seen him.

There have been other sightings, too: near Reydon Hall, on the road between Middleton in Essex and Boxford in Suffolk, at Wicken Fen near Newmarket and on the Cromer to Aldeburgh coast road. MacGregor relates that one evening at the turn of the century a Southwold couple were driving home near Reydon Hall when Black Shuck appeared almost under the horses' hooves. But when the driver hit out at it with his whip to frighten it off, concerned that they might run over it, 'it just wasn't there any longer.'

But one of the most frightening encounters happened during the last war. An American airman and his wife had rented a flat-topped hut on the edge of Walberswick Marsh while the husband was serving at the nearby airbase. One evening during a bad storm they suddenly heard loud pounding on the door, and when the airman looked through the window, he was amazed to see a huge black dog repeatedly hurling its body at their hut.

It must have seemed an incredible nightmare, but as it went on the couple piled whatever furniture they had against the door, becoming terrified as the creature still continued to batter the hut walls, and even jumped up onto the flat roof.

Their ordeal continued for some hours, but as dawn arrived at last and the noise ceased, they cautiously emerged to inspect the damage. To their amazement there was no evidence of the ferocious battering of the night before, and no paw marks in the soft mud round the hut.

Alasdair Alpin MacGregor also described another Walberswick inhabitant's sighting of 'the terrible monster of the Common'. She and her sister-in-law saw 'a phantom dog the size of a calf' and said that on stormy nights it had often been both seen and heard on its travels between Aldeburgh and Cromer.

But the most unforgettable Black Dog case dates back many centuries to 4th August 1577 when 'a Straunge and terrible Wunder' befell the churches of Bungay and Blythburgh. During morning service at St Mary's church, Bungay, an unusually violent storm was raging outside when the service was disrupted as a huge black dog burst in surrounded by lightning flashes. It swept through the building 'with greate swiftnesse and incredible haste among the people' and when it passed between two of the worshippers, according to the old 16th-century tract, it 'wrung the necks of them bothe at one instant clene backward insomuch that, even at a moment where they kneeled, they straungely died'. Another unfortunate man survived, but was shrivelled up 'like a piece of leather scorched in a hot fire'.

This creature, believed by the people to have been the Devil in the form of Black Shuck, also burst upon the congregation at Blythburgh church on the same day, killing two men and a young lad and leaving his trademark in the form of deep black marks, said to be claw marks, on the north door, which can still be seen. Bungay's memento is in the form of a Black Dog weathervane in the town centre.

As well as the Black Dog's fearsome appearance, people say there is a sulphurous smell and when places where it has appeared are examined, a smell of brimstone is noticed and the ground appears to be scorched. Small wonder then, that Black Dogs are believed to be creatures of the Devil, if not the Devil himself in the form of a dog.

Another supernatural creature with some resemblance to Black Shuck is known as the Shug Monkey, sometimes seen nearby in Cambridgeshire in a lane called Slough Hill on the road between West Wratting and Balsham. A witness described it as 'a cross between a big rough coated dog and a monkey with big shining eyes. Sometimes it would shuffle along on its hind legs and at other times it would whizz past on all fours'.

These days we hear more about sightings of large black cats than black dogs. There is something almost supernatural about those reported glimpses of an unusual beast spotted in the distance or appearing in the car headlights and vanishing just as suddenly. Could some of them have been our old friend Black Shuck? It's said he has his roots in the Hound of Odin whose Norse legend arrived on our shores with the Viking invasion. And certainly he is one of the oldest and most terrifying reported phantoms known in this country.

9

The Phantom Fliers

DURING the Second World War airfields were built all over East Anglia from which RAF and USAAF bombers and fighter planes flew the Channel on their dangerous missions, and inevitably some never returned, while others just managed to limp home on a wing and a prayer.

Perhaps it is not surprising that many of these former airfields have their stories of mysterious happenings – the sound of aircraft in an empty sky, figures in uniform or flying gear who disappear as suddenly as they come, and others, apparently of flesh and blood, who hitch a lift only to vanish unexpectedly.

In 1951 an American security policeman was driving round Lakenheath Air Force Base at night when he noticed an RAF pilot in uniform at the side of the road waiting for a lift. He stopped and the man got in, and soon afterwards asked the driver if he had a cigarette. The policeman passed him a cigarette and when asked for a light handed over his lighter.

As he stopped at a checkpoint to get clearance to proceed further, out of the corner of his eye he registered the flick of the lighter, then turned towards the passenger only to find the seat empty, with the lighter lying there!

Not long ago a man travelling to work from Felixstowe to Ipswich early one morning paused at some traffic lights, then as he set off again he noticed whistling which seemed to come from inside his car. He glanced in his mirror and was astonished to see an RAF officer sitting on the back seat, unconcernedly whistling away!

He drew up and opened the rear door and spoke to the figure dressed in a pilot's leather flying jacket, but there was no response. He didn't know what to do, so got back in and continued, his passenger still whistling. The driver realised that there was something uncanny about his mysterious passenger, and when he got to work he hastily parked his car and hurried into the factory without a backward glance. He decided not to tell any of his workmates what had happened in case they laughed at him, but he was not looking forward to the homeward journey.

However, when the time came, to his relief the car was empty and he set off for home. But he had scarcely travelled half a mile when he heard whistling, and a scared glance in the mirror told him that the pilot was there again, sitting on the back seat.

Nearing home, he reached the same set of traffic lights where the pilot had first made his appearance that morning, and while he paused at the lights the whistling stopped, and a glance in the mirror told him that the back seat was now empty!

But this was not the end of it! Every day for a week the same thing happened, the pilot appearing in the car just past that particular set of traffic lights and disappearing there on the homeward journey. And every day he whistled the same tune! Apart from the weirdness of it all, that tune was driving the driver crazy. Something had to be done.

Fortunately there was another route he could take, although it was longer. He decided to give it a try and, to his relief, on the new route there was no sign of the phantom whistler. After a month, he thought he might risk a return to his old journey to work, and he approached the traffic lights at the crossroads with some trepidation. But luck was with him, the lights were green, so he drove straight across realising thankfully that there was no sign of his unwelcome passenger. In fact he was so delighted to be back to normal that he started to whistle lightheartedly, and realised he was whistling That Tune! However, although the pilot's tune continued to haunt him for some time, there was never again any sign of his ghostly passenger.

The old airbase at Martlesham Heath became the site of Suffolk Police Headquarters and various business premises after the war and in 1981 the local *Star* newspaper reported that one of the police had seen the ghost of an RAF pilot in flying gear. Apparently during a spell of leisure he had been playing with a fruit machine when he realised that someone was watching him. But as he looked up, he had scarcely registered the airman's presence when the figure vanished.

The story inspired a number of letters to the paper, one describing a similar incident at another business on the site. An employee was working on a word processor one Sunday morning when he too had the sensation of being watched. He looked up to find a man in RAF uniform standing in the doorway, apparently very interested in the computer, who then turned and walked away quickly down a corridor.

The employee knew that the door at the end of the corridor was locked, forming a dead end, but when he followed the intruder he found the corridor empty. He looked all round the building and found no one, and the outer doors were still locked.

There was yet another sighting of what seems to have been the same figure which appeared in another building on the site when a man was playing the piano. Again he looked up to find an airman watching him, who, on being noticed, disappeared without trace.

It was suggested by other correspondents that the ghost could date back to before the Second World War. Someone who served at RAF Martlesham Heath in the 1930s said that in those days the airfield already had a reputation for being haunted, and he and other servicemen always tried to avoid doing guard duty on B Flight Road. Around two or three in the morning a strange atmosphere would build up which they found frightening, and the rumour was that the ghost was a parachutist named 'Brainy' Dobbs who was killed in the late 1920s. Some thought that Dobbs Lane in Kesgrave was named after the airman.

Mr Gordon Kinsey who wrote a history of RAF Martlesham Heath confirmed that Leading Aircraftman Ernest 'Brainy' Dobbs had been a well-known personality in the Parachute Experimental Section. He was a colourful character with a devil-may-care reputation, notorious for his various hare-brained inventions, who tragically came to grief while demonstrating jumping with huge balloons over obstacles at Hendon, when he failed to clear some high tension electric cables and was killed.

As for Dobbs Lane, Kesgrave, it is said to be named after John Dobbs (1684–1722) who hanged himself after the death of his wife in childbirth. He was buried in the lane as in those days suicides could not be interred in consecrated ground and his ghost is said to have haunted there ever since. Rumour has it that in 1936 a few drunken revellers opened the grave and removed some bones as mementoes, but fled in terror when a ghostly white figure appeared out of the trees.

So who is the ghost of the former Martlesham Heath airfield? The policeman who encountered the apparition in

1982 described a man aged about 40–45 with dark swept-back hair and a ruddy complexion. But people who remember 'Brainy' Dobbs describe him as practically bald. It seems likely that the ghost's identity will remain a mystery.

Former airfields of the 1939–1945 war still sometimes seem to retain memories of those days even when traces of their wartime activities are long gone. The site of the large American Air Force base at Langham became an apple orchard, but workers there have often reported the sounds of unseen aircraft zooming in low over the trees, sometimes followed by the sickening sound of a crash landing. And the shadowy figures of airmen in flying kit have been seen wandering as if dazed among the apple trees, but when any attempt is made to approach them they fade away.

And at Parham disused airfield where the droning of returning aircraft was sometimes heard, the old control tower had a reputation for being haunted. When the tower was being turned into a museum commemorating 390 Bomber Group, US Eighth Air Force, a man was checking it for damp one stormy night when, while he was upstairs, another set of wet footprints mysteriously appeared beside his own. 'They walked in and turned round through an old doorway that has now been removed, then stopped in the middle of the room,' he said.

As he was alone in the building, it seemed decidedly eerie.

'A couple of nights later we went to view a collection of Eighth Air Force uniforms and I saw some flying boots,' he went on. 'The sole impression was exactly the same as the one on the floor. Up to then I had been very sceptical about the stories, but that frightened me to such a degree that I won't stay there on my own now.'

Someone else working on the tower remarked that one morning when he opened the place up he was surprised to notice the smell of fresh cigar smoke, although the building was empty.

'Someone is keeping an eye on us to see what we are doing, but it is nothing malevolent,' he said.

These old airfields have seen so much courage and camaraderie coupled with tragedy and loss, it is small wonder that echoes linger and shadows seem almost tangible. The memories will never be forgotten.

10

Bury's Ghostly Monks and Others

ANYONE who knows Bury St Edmunds will not be surprised that writer M.R. James described it as 'the most attractive town in Suffolk'. William Cobbett went further. To him it was 'The nicest town in the world', and when Dickens stayed at the old Angel Hotel while giving readings at the Athenaeum, he thought it a handsome little town.

The great Abbey which once dominated the town is now just a ruin set in public gardens beyond the massive Abbey gateway but echoes of the days when it was all powerful remain in the remarkable number of ghostly monks reported all over the town including around the gateway of the Abbey itself. This area has been described as one of the most spiritually powerful spots in England and the long distance alignment of ley lines known as the St Michael's Line which links many significant ancient sites touches Bury St Edmunds.

Abbeygate Street opposite the Abbey has cellars beneath the shops with archways, which may originally have been the Abbey's wine cellars, and it is thought that tunnels ran from the Abbey to many of the old buildings nearby.

It is here that shop employees have sometimes seen shadowy monks glide by. The manager of a corn

61

merchants in Abbeygate Street was working late one night upstairs when he felt something brush past his shoulder, and when he turned round he saw 'a big fat monk in brown robes, with a girdle round him and a black cap on his head.'

The manager tried to speak but couldn't, and when the ghost moved away he followed and saw it pass along the landing and then disappear.

At a bakery in the same street in 1980, a monk was seen standing in front of the dishwasher, and the cooking rings on the ovens would switch themselves on and off at times for no apparent reason. Several other shops have reported sightings of monks over the years, also footsteps and other unexplained sounds.

Bury claims to have Britain's smallest pub, the Nutshell in Abbeygate, where a ghostly monk has also been seen. In the late 1980s there was the sound of a crying child in the glass store upstairs, and in the cellar the fragrant scent of perfume comes and goes.

Said to be linked to the Nutshell by a tunnel is Cupola House Hotel, originally built as a private house in the 17th century. It bears a plaque to Daniel Defoe, who may have lived or stayed there when he visited Bury in 1704. Stories of a ghostly grey lady at Cupola House date back centuries and she is said to haunt the tunnel and cellars. Perhaps she finds it lonely down there as sometimes she has been seen sitting in the corner of the front bar.

The Priory Hotel in Tollgate Lane has all the necessary qualifications for a haunted building as part of it was built over the burial ground of a medieval friary. When archaeologists excavated the site of a chapel they discovered a priest's coffin complete with skeleton. There is a haunted bedroom, much in demand with hopeful ghost hunters, said to have a 'chilling presence'.

Yet another hotel in the town is the Suffolk with yet another monk seen in yet another tunnel. It is built on the site of a much older inn and the tunnel formed a link between it and a priory nearby which was destroyed in the time of Henry VIII.

Bury also has the delightful Regency Theatre Royal, its auditorium decorated in a rich dark red, the boxes adorned with angels and winged beasts in gold, and the ceiling a charmingly painted view of the cloudy heavens. Altogether an enchanting place, but I had visited it hoping to hear something about its ghost.

He is said to be William Wilkins who built the theatre in 1819, an architect also remembered for his work on London's National Gallery. Unfortunately by 1830 Wilkins was in financial difficulties and his theatre closed in 1843. It was reopened in 1845 by William Abington, and it's said that sorrow at his own failure is the reason why Wilkins' sad wraith haunts the theatre.

However, no one there seemed to have any knowledge of his presence in recent times, so perhaps the present-day success of his charming little theatre has calmed his restless spirit.

11

Trouble at the Mill

WE visited Letheringham Watermill on the only fine day in the torrentially wet and cold Easter of 1998. The old white-painted mill and mill house stand by the river at the end of a narrow lane forming the kind of picture Constable might have liked to paint, and the garden on different levels is patrolled majestically by peacocks.

It seemed to me a magical spot, difficult to associate with the dark and dreadful deeds that once shocked that peaceful countryside.

A mill was recorded here in the Domesday Book and successive owners have rebuilt and modified it on the same site. The present building dates from 1740, but before that, in 1696, the mill was the scene of a dreadful crime. The miller at that time was John Bullard, and he and his son were working together on their accounts when a journeyman, Jonah Snell, a temporary employee of theirs, murdered them both with an axe.

It is said that afterwards he hung their bodies upside down from a beam in the mill. What was the motive for such a hideous crime? Perhaps if they were doing accounts they were handling money and robbery was in Jonah Snell's evil mind when he crept into the mill and took the two men by surprise. But instead of making his getaway before he was discovered he performed the macabre task of hanging up the bodies, and possibly this was how he came to be caught.

At any rate, caught he was, and taken for trial at Wickham Market, where he was found guilty and hanged on a gibbet at Potsford, where his body was left to swing in chains until it rotted away, after the gruesome custom of the times.

As I stood on an upper floor at the mill watching the wheel turning with the sun streaming through the window and outside the river running through banks full of daffodils, I remembered I'd been told that in 1994 a lady visiting the mill with a coach party had had a frightening experience. She had looked up and clearly seen the apparition of a figure hanging from a beam inside the mill. Was it a supernatural vision of three hundred years ago when the murderer Snell hung up his victims' bodies in the mill which preceded the present building?

Psychic research groups have found the atmosphere at night can be quite disturbing for the sensitive. An ancient area like this with a long history is bound to be full of memories and, possibly, ghosts. There is evidence that a wooden church stood close by the mill in Saxon times, but although the building itself has long gone, old human bones have often come to light during work in the mill gardens over the past two centuries, perhaps from the graveyard of the old church.

As recently as 1987 during the great hurricane which destroyed many mature trees, four complete skeletons were discovered under the roots of a fallen tree near the mill house. But the present owners take this evidence of former occupation quite calmly.

'They are very friendly bones,' they say.

Not far away on the B1078 road is Potsford Wood where, during tree felling work in 1958, the remains of the old gibbet were found and re-erected. This is where the murderer Jonah Snell was hanged, and the gibbet with a plaque is still there. The place has an eerie reputation locally and as recently as 1997 a couple were driving late at night along the road past Potsford when their car broke down. They decided to walk up Draggards Hill to find a phone box, but as they passed the gibbet site they noticed what appeared to be lights in the wood.

They thought that possibly there was a house nearby where they could phone, and entered the wood, pausing to look at the plaque by the gibbet. But as they stood there they heard a queer moaning noise and, thinking it could be someone trying to frighten them, they walked back to the gate. Looking back towards the gibbet they saw something strange which appeared to be a black 'blob' moving about.

Not surprisingly they were glad to get back to the car, and even more relieved when another motorist stopped to see if he could help them. He turned out to be an off duty policeman, and when they told him about their experience in the wood, he did not seem surprised.

He told them that in the 1980s a lorry driver passing along the same stretch of road drew up and went into the wood to relieve himself. Like the couple, he too noticed the old gibbet and had paused to read the plaque when he felt a tap on his shoulder. One can imagine his horrified reactions when he turned to see a black-cloaked figure standing behind him, and beneath the hood no face, but the skull of a skeleton!

Heart pounding, he fled for his life, jumped into his lorry and drove off at breakneck speed. This happening seems almost reminiscent of a Hammer Horror movie, but it was broad daylight, not midnight, and the man concerned had stopped there by chance and knew nothing about this creepy site.

The stories seem to date back to 1958 when the old gibbet was re-erected. Not surprisingly there are other gibbet sites with eerie reputations, such as the place where Black Toby met his end at Blythburgh and in Hertfordshire a huge shaggy black dog haunts Gubblecote Cross, near Long Marston, believed to be the ghost of Thomas Colley, hanged there in 1751 for murdering an old woman by 'swimming' her as a witch.

It seems that even after hundreds of years evil or tragic events still leave their traces, and someone in the wrong place at the wrong time may experience a disturbing brush with the supernatural.

12

Strange Visitors

The Green Children

THE delightful village of Woolpit is a fascinating place. The church has a wonderful angel roof with over 200 carved wooden angels, their wings outspread above the congregation. And its village sign commemorates one of the strangest folk tales in medieval history, the coming of the two green children.

The sign also shows a wolf, and some say the pits in the area are where captured wolves were once thrown to die, hence the village's name. It is also possible that these pits are originally where the Romans excavated the deposits of brick earth, used for the white bricks for which Woolpit is known.

If you visit the interesting little Bygones Museum in the village you can find a translation of William of Newburgh's chronicle of a strange event which dates back more than 800 years – and is as mysterious today as on that day at harvest-time during the reign of King Stephen (1135–1154) when something happened in Woolpit that has never been forgotten.

The story was chronicled both by Ralph, Abbot of Coggleshall, and William of Newburgh and tells how the farm workers looked up from their harvesting to see two small figures emerging from the nearby pits. To the astonishment of the harvesters, the girl and boy had completely green skin, and were wearing unusual clothes. They seemed unable to understand what was said to them, and their own speech was unintelligible to the farm workers who took them to the village where they were a source of much curiosity and amazement.

They were taken to stay at the house of the local landowner, Sir Richard de Calne, where they refused to eat any of the food offered them, although they were obviously very hungry. But when some green beans were brought in, they ate these avidly and for a time would eat nothing else. Eventually the children were baptised but the boy, who seemed frail and depressed, did not survive for long. The girl adapted to a normal diet and her skin eventually changed to a healthy colour, and, says William of Newburgh, she became 'not much different from our own women'.

She soon picked up the English language and was able to answer the many questions everyone was longing to ask. She said that they had come from the land of St Martin. The sun didn't rise there and they lived in perpetual twilight but they could see another 'land of light' across a big river. She and her brother had been looking after their father's flocks in the fields when they heard the sound of some beautiful bells such as those of the great abbey of St Edmund, and they had entered an underground passageway in search of them and eventually emerged into bright dazzling sunlight where the harvesters found them.

William of Newburgh's account differs in that the children heard a great noise and whilst they were wondering about it, they suddenly found themselves among the harvesters in strange surroundings. This version almost suggests that the children were unexpectedly transported to Woolpit by some means. He also commented reasonably enough that this story was too complicated for our intelligence to understand, but needless to say there have been many attempts to solve the mystery of the green children.

There is a village called Fornham St Martin not far from Woolpit, close to the river Lark, could this have been the children's 'St Martin's land'? If so, when the girl became older, surely she might have tried to return home there.

The green children's story has been linked with another familiar legend, the 'Babes in the Wood'. This relates how two children, on the death of their parents, were left in the care of their wicked uncle, a medieval Norfolk earl, who had his eye on their inheritance. He tried to poison them with arsenic (which incidentally can cause the skin to turn green) and when this did not work, he sent the children into Wayland Wood in the Thetford Forest area accompanied by two henchmen, with instructions to put them to death. However, one of the men had a change of heart and killed his companion who was intent on murdering the children. The children were then left in the dark forest to wander hopelessly lost until, exhausted, they lay down beneath a tree together and died.

Possibly, far from being children from a rich aristocratic family like the Babes in the Wood, the green children could have belonged to paupers, living rough in the forest on a poor diet which might have caused them to have an anaemic greenish skin colour. And the perpetual leafy darkness of the forest could account for the twilight world they described. And once in the comfort of Sir Richard de Calne's home, where the girl later became a maidservant, she found herself so much better off that she had no wish to return to her previous miserable surroundings. Descriptions of her suggest that she was a lively character who may have deliberately mystified her questioners about her origins.

This scenario sounds quite plausible, and yet the shocked amazement with which the farm workers greeted their appearance suggests that their colouring was dramatically green, and some accounts say that their clothing was green too, of a style and material quite unfamiliar to the Woolpit villagers.

So who were the green children? Aliens? Visitors from a parallel universe or even from the land of fairies, green being a colour associated with the fairy world?

After more than eight hundred years, is there anything new to be said about the green children? Surprisingly enough, there is. At the *Fortean Times* magazine's Unconvention held in London in 1997 a talk was given by Duncan Lunan who has extensively researched the subject. He disagrees that the green children arrived during the reign of King Stephen as Ralph of Coggleshall had the story first hand from Richard de Calne himself, and he considers that Ralph could not have been at Coggleshall much before 1180, so the children are more likely to have come during the reign of Henry II.

While looking at the family tree of the de Calnes, Lunan found that Sybilla, Richard de Calne's orphaned granddaughter, was his only female heir, but he also found mention of another woman, older than Sybilla, who jointly inherited some property. Her name was Agnes, no surname, and Lunan believes there is a strong possibility that Agnes was the green girl who had been a member of Richard de Calne's household since she arrived in Woolpit.

In 1180 Agnes married Richard Barre, one of the king's senior ambassadors, but she had already had an illegitimate son by him, born in 1177/8, followed by a legitimate son in 1184. Agnes lived until her eighties in the Barre estate in Staffordshire. This, of course, differs completely from the usual story that the green girl grew up and married a man from Kings Lynn.

In his *Anatomy of Melancholy*, Richard Burton conjectures that the green children may have come from Mars or Venus, an attractive but unlikely theory. But since there is nowhere on this globe that fits the dark world they described, inhabited by people as green as themselves, were they aliens somehow teleported from another planet? Or were they more prosaically just lost children from Fornham St Martin?

However, that still leaves the main mystery unsolved. Why were they green? Duncan Lunan points out that Agnes Barre has descendants alive today, and if she was the green girl, DNA testing of one of them might provide interesting revelations!

As William of Newburgh admitted, the mystery of the green children was something he could not understand or fathom with any concentration of his mind. And that goes for me too.

Visitors from the Sea

ORFORD today has little to remind the visitor of the prosperous port it once was, except the castle Henry II built in 1165 as a stronghold against the treacherous Hugh Bigod of Bungay.

Some forty years after the castle was built, in or around 1204, Orford was buzzing with excitement. Ralph of Coggleshall, the abbot chronicler, always pleased to spice up his history with something strange and curious, included an account of the day when some Orford fishermen found in their nets the most remarkable catch of their lives.

As they pulled on their nets, the men realised that they

had an unusually heavy catch. It took all their strength to haul it aboard and when they did they gazed in bewilderment at the creature tangled in the nets among the fish. There, staring angrily back at them, was a man with a long straggly beard and naked hairy body, the crown of his head almost bald.

The fishermen hauled him off to the custodian of Orford Castle, Bartholomew de Gladville, who kept him prisoner and persistently tried to communicate with his strange captive. But apart from a few noises the wild man had nothing to say. They gave him raw fish and watched as he squeezed out the moisture with his hands before eating it. But when they became frustrated at the wild man's silence, they even tortured him by hanging him up by his ankles but had to accept at last that he was unable to understand them or answer their questions, and when he was taken to Orford's Norman church it was obvious that the religious service meant absolutely nothing to him.

One day nets were stretched across the harbour so that the wild man could enjoy a swim, but he escaped easily by diving beneath the nets and was soon well out to sea, diving and leaping out of the water in a display which obviously said 'Catch me if you can'. His captors thought that was probably the last they would ever see of him, but before long he returned to Orford of his own accord. There he remained for a time, but no doubt the call of the sea was too strong and one day he slipped away back to his life beneath the waves and Orford saw him no more.

Was the story of the Orford wild man true or a legend? There is so much detail that, strange as it seems, it could well be authentic. In any case, this is not the only mysterious sea creature to haunt the East Anglian coast.

For centuries there have been tales of a Nessie-like serpent seen in the sea at Kessingland. In his book *The*

Supernatural Coast Peter Haining reports several sightings. There is an account in *The Gentleman's Magazine* in 1750 of a creature about five feet long 'from what could be viewed of it above the water', with a head like a dog and a beard like a lion. Other sightings were reported in the 19th century of a sea monster with a serpent-like head and humps behind.

But in July 1912 a really full and exciting account of the creature arrived in a letter to the well-known author Sir Henry Rider Haggard from his daughter Lilias, who was staying at the family's seaside house, Kessingland Grange.

The house on the cliff edge had once been a coastguard station and had an excellent view of the sea, and Lilias and two friends were sitting on the lawn when they noticed something resembling a thin dark line 'with a blob at one end' shooting through the water at a tremendous speed. She hurried to get a pair of binoculars and although the object was almost out of sight she could distinguish a head followed by a series of about thirty pointed 'blobs'. Lilias estimated that it was about thirty feet long.

Rider Haggard was working at his house at Ditchingham not far away and was so excited by his daughter's news that he set off straight away to Kessingland. Lilias, still thrilled by what she had seen, regaled her father again with the details, and the servants at the house assured him that there had been talk for years of the strange sea serpent which turned up in the sea off Kessingland in the summer.

Rider Haggard wrote to the *Eastern Daily Press* to ask if anyone else had seen Lilias's serpent, and although there were many suggestions that it had been a trick of the light, a sandbank suddenly exposed or a school of porpoises or dolphins, others less sceptical remembered previous stories of the Kessingland sea serpent.

As recently as July 1978 a holidaymaker walking towards Covehithe noticed a long neck suddenly appear out of the sea with a series of humps behind. He described it in the *East Anglian Magazine* as having a head like a seal, and it disappeared beneath the waves so quickly that he said he would have thought he had imagined this unusual sighting if he had not read the story of the Kessingland serpent.

What other strange visitors are beneath the waters off the Suffolk coast, one wonders, waiting to be seen?

13

The Mystery of the Bells

ONE of Suffolk's best known and mysterious manifestations of the paranormal occurred in 1834 at the lovely old Georgian property Great Bealings House near Woodbridge.

From 2nd February 1834 until 27th March the same year, the bells in the house rang intermittently of their own accord, or so it appeared, and the occupant of the house, Major Edward Moor, kept a meticulous record of the curious series of events which remain as inexplicable today as they were at the time.

It began on Sunday afternoon, 2nd February 1834, when the dining room bell rang three times at intervals, surprising the two servants in the house as no one else was there to ring it! However, although they reported the odd happening to Major Moor when he came in, it would soon have been forgotten if nothing else had followed.

However, next day during the afternoon the same bell rang several times, Major Moor arriving home shortly before 5 pm in time to hear the last peal.

The day after (Tuesday) produced a positive cacophony and Major Moor's return at 5 pm was greeted by the servants with the news that all the bells in the kitchen had been ringing violently. As if to confirm it, the Major heard a loud peal and hurried to the kitchen where the cook said that five of the nine bells hanging there in a row had been ringing constantly every quarter of an hour. And as the Major and his son and two servants stood looking at the bells, the same five bells rang so violently that it seemed as if they might be shaken from their fastenings.

Startled by this, Major Moor continued to watch the bells and, sure enough, after about ten minutes another noisy carillon rang out, although it seemed not quite so loud as before. And after another quarter of an hour, the same five bells rang again. These bells were those for the dining room, the drawing room above it, an adjacent bedroom and two attics over the drawing room.

That same day during dinner in what was known as the bréakfast room, the bell from there rang although no one was near the bell pull, and down in the kitchen where the six servants were having dinner, the five bells which had rung so frequently before now continued to peal every few minutes and continued at lengthening intervals until 7.45 pm, finishing with just one solitary ring from a bell which was wired to an attic.

The bells in the house had been installed in 1806, and apart from the wire of one bell being replaced, none had needed attention, and their extraordinary behaviour was so inexplicable that Major Moor was convinced that no human agency was involved.

On Wednesday, 5th February, there were more peals from the bells, and one bell rang so violently that the strip of iron from which it was suspended actually struck the ceiling.

Determined to get to the bottom of the puzzle, Major Moor sent a servant to go round the house pulling the bell pulls one by one while he was in the kitchen. He saw that the bells responded quite normally, unlike the frenzied violence when they rang of their own accord.

The Major, still baffled, was away in Woodbridge for the afternoon, and found on his return that there had been more intermittent ringing.

But after this, to the relief of everyone at Great Bealings House, there was a lull. Major Moor wrote an account of what had occurred to the *Ipswich Journal* and discussed the happening with various gentlemen of his acquaintance, and they and sundry readers of the newspaper all offered a variety of solutions. But the Major did not possess a mischievous monkey, the house was not rat or mice infested, and the wires to the bells were visible along their entire course except where they passed through holes in the walls.

Trickery was of course suggested, but Major Moor dismissed the possibility and declared that no one who had witnessed the phenomenon could believe it had been achieved by tricks. He had examined the wiring of the bells indoors and out without finding anything wrong, and had witnessed the bells ringing when everyone in the house was present and he was satisfied that no living person was responsible.

But the peace of Great Bealings House was shortlived. On the afternoon of 15th March when Major Moor arrived home he was greeted with the news that the bells were ringing again. Apparently the same five bells which had been the noisiest had set up a violent peal when the butler was alone in the house that afternoon and twenty minutes later when three servants were in the kitchen, the bells rang again. A neighbour was present when, about three-quarters of an hour later, there was another peal, followed by a final solitary ring from the bell of the best bedroom.

A few days later while the Major was in London, his son wrote to tell him that on 22nd March the five most active bells had sounded again. Curiously enough, a local schoolmaster was in the kitchen discussing the subject with the cook, and when he remarked that he wished he could hear them, the bells obliged!

On 27th March there were a couple of peals from the bells during the afternoon, but that was their swan song. From then on there was no more spontaneous bell ringing at Great Bealings House.

At the suggestion of a friend, Major Moor wrote an account of these strange happenings and a small book was published and sold to raise money for a new church at Woodbridge. He included a few other reports of unexplained bell ringing elsewhere, but nothing as prolonged and persistent as the mysterious behaviour of his own bells. Was there some natural but undiscovered explanation, or was there some ghostly hand on the bell pulls? Like Major Moor, I am baffled.

At Christmas 1951 Alasdair Alpin MacGregor, the well-known writer on ghosts, described in *The Sphere* magazine a recent visit to Great Bealings House when he was told by the owner that the house was haunted by a little old lady in grey, sometimes seen tripping silently in and out of the powder closet off one of the bedrooms.

He was also told of a recent strange visitant to nearby Rosery Cottage, home of the groom and his wife. While they were both sitting by the fire one evening they heard footsteps on the path outside. Mrs Crafer looked out of the window and just glimpsed the side view of a man who appeared to be walking round the house to the front door. But no one arrived there, and when she looked there was no one about at all.

A few months later when Mr and Mrs Crafer were both indoors they heard footsteps outside and both saw the side face, head and cap of a man passing the window. 'That's the same man I saw go past the window before,' said Mrs Crafer, and when no one arrived at the front door she ran upstairs and looked out of the window from where she had an uninterrupted view of their garden and surrounding area. And yet again there was no sign of the mysterious caller who never arrived!

14

Ghosts Galore

Newmarket

ALTHOUGH he died more than a hundred years ago, Fred Archer is still remembered as one of the most famous jockeys of all time. He rode the Derby winner five times and won fifteen other classic races.

He was only 29 when he died, and was said to have been inconsolable after the death of his young wife only a year after their marriage.

Newmarket has a reputation for many unexplained accidents on the racecourse which are attributed to Archer's ghost. Horses have often appeared frightened, causing them to swerve unexpectedly or slow down. Some have stumbled or fallen, but when the ground is examined nothing is found to account for it.

In 1927 a local woman and her daughter saw a grey horse and rider emerge from a copse and approach them. There was no sound and the woman was convinced that she had seen the ghost of Archer, whom she recognised. Other people confirmed that they, too, had seen the ghostly horse and rider in the Hamilton Stud Lane area, and also on the heath.

In 1950 the Aga Khan's horse, Kermanshah, fell in a race, and the jockey, Charlie Smirke, said the horse had seemed to stumble although he could see nothing to account for it. But, oddly enough, a horse called Excalibur had fallen at the same spot a year before. And jockeys and members of the public have sometimes noticed a white misty shape hovering in the air there.

The Gypsy's Grave

TRADITIONALLY suicides were buried at crossroads, and near Kentford, not far from Newmarket, on the B1506, is one of the best known crossroads burials. The Gypsy's Grave, as it is called, is easily seen by the side of the road, marked by a wooden cross. When I visited the spot while writing this book there was a stone vase which held carnations, now withered, and lots of artificial flowers. And people had rather strangely thrown coins on the grave.

The story is that the grave contains the body of a young gypsy boy who was minding sheep and when he found that some of his flock were missing, in fear of the consequences, he took his own life. Another version says that he was falsely accused of sheep stealing, for which the penalty was death, so he hanged himself. There is a local superstition that the flowers on the grave on Derby Day foretell the winner's colours.

Ghosts at the Rectory

POLSTEAD village is well-known for its association with the famous Murder in the Red Barn, but there is another macabre story from the area, this time concerning the large, rambling 16th-century rectory.

It was in the spring of 1978 that a new Rector, the Rev Hayden Foster, his wife Margo and their baby son arrived at their new home. All was well until the fifth night when visitors joined them for his induction due to take place the following day, and the Fosters moved out of their bedroom into another one in order to accommodate their guests.

That night Margo Foster woke at about 3 am experiencing a feeling of terror as to her alarm she saw the freshly painted walls of the room change before her eyes to peeling damp old wallpaper. She heard a child's scream, but was certain it was not her own child, Gerard, and felt as if something was trying to suffocate or strangle her.

The couple were terrified, and said afterwards that if anyone had asked them beforehand if they believed in ghosts they would have said 'No'.

'But we certainly believe in something now,' said Mr Foster. 'There is a definite feeling of evil in that place.'

Mrs Foster had tried to say the Lord's Prayer but was unable to get the words out due to what she described as an overwhelming force, and her husband felt there had been real danger in the room. Unable to face spending another night in the rectory the family moved out to stay with friends the following morning, and for some time subsequently felt the effects of their experience. For weeks afterwards their little boy woke at night screaming, and Mrs Foster needed medical care.

The Bishop of St Edmundsbury and Ipswich at the time remembered that there had been an exorcism at the rectory about seven years before in a bid to drive out 'evil spirits', but assuming it had been effective, no one had anticipated that the Fosters would be subjected to their night of terror.

Apparently the rectory's history of paranormal happenings dated back a long way as it was found that the Rev John Whitmore who was Rector at Polstead from 1795 to 1840 performed an exorcism at the beginning of the 19th century.

Mrs Mary Neads, widow of a former Rector, said there

were several unexplained happenings during the sixteen years that she lived at the rectory. 'I never saw anything, but we heard heavy steps coming up the stairs about 11.30 one night, and several times we heard people coming down the gravel drive and found there was no one there when we went to greet them,' she said. But apparently she and her husband got quite used to it.

'When we heard the footsteps we'd just say, "There they are, going upstairs again." There are places where these things happen, and it isn't always unpleasant. I know some people who have seen ghosts and like them a lot,' she said.

But apparently during the time of the Rev Paul Biddle-combe, who was Rector before 1963, there were what was described as 'unfortunate and unexplained incidents'.

After the Fosters left the rectory, the Church wisely decided that, haunting apart, the property was too big and expensive to run and it was put on the market with its sixteen rooms, large garden and paddock, and dark history.

The house was bought in 1979 and renovated by a family said to be sceptical about the hauntings. Apparently they, too, have heard the sound of wheels on the gravel drive when there is nothing to account for it, and sometimes there is a curious unidentifiable smell which comes and goes.

Once when some workmen were replacing the roof, one of them apologised for disturbing a person seen in an attic room. Apparently someone with long white hair had turned away from the window, seemingly annoyed at his presence, but when the house owner told them there was no one there, the workman felt 'a bit ill', and couldn't continue what he was doing.

But, fortunately, there has been no recurrence of the

Fosters' nightmare experience for the family in residence and they seem quite happy to share their home with whatever ghosts there may be.

Mystery at the Museum

CHRISTCHURCH Mansion, a 500 year old building in Ipswich dating back to Tudor times, is now open to the public with its important collection of paintings and sculpture, furniture and ceramics. With its charming stately home atmosphere, it would not be surprising to find that essential of the best stately homes, a legendary ghost or two prowling the corridors or drifting mysteriously through the venerable walls.

In the summer of 1995 the local press reported some eerie goings-on disturbing the calm of the Mansion. Floorboards were creaking and unexplained footsteps were heard, books were launched across the room by an unseen hand, and pictures fell down for no obvious reason.

A night watchman said nervously, 'There is definitely something or somebody here,' and the daytime security guard, while admitting that he had never seen a ghost in the house, said that he had actually witnessed pictures fall slowly down the wall, furniture move of its own accord and a book fly across the room.

A woman visiting the Mansion with her young daughter was alarmed to see a female figure sweep past them and disappear straight through a glass door without opening it! She said she saw a lady dressed in white with a bonnet in the Victorian bedroom who moved on into the Victorian parlour, and as the figure passed by the air went very cold.

There is a legend that a young maid became pregnant by one of the Mansion's owners more than 200 years ago, and she was murdered by being thrown down the stairs. Obviously this tragedy, if true, could have something to do with the haunting.

While researching in Ipswich Record Office I came across a happier ghost story concerning the Mansion. Apparently before the building became a museum, a young housemaid employed by the Fonnereau family turned a corner into a long first floor corridor and saw ahead of her a young woman dancing along with a small child clinging to each hand. The happy trio were laughing lightheartedly and the maid who saw them was puzzled as she knew they were neither members of the family nor guests. She also noticed that their clothes were of a much earlier period.

When she mentioned what had happened she found that this rather delightful haunting was quite calmly accepted by the household, and she herself saw the happy little trio again several times after that.

It doesn't seem likely that there is any connection between these hauntings, both echoes of an old house's long and varied history.

The Ghost that Wasn't

IN Lowestoft apparently they still remember the famous Clapham Road Ghost. It seems that some thirty or forty years ago this ghost was the talk of Lowestoft and attracted a nightly crowd of watchers eager to have their blood chilled by a sighting of the fearsome phantom.

At times the police even had to step in to persuade the eager ghost hunters to go home.

'Us boys used to be up there every night watching for it,' recalled a resident, 'it was a dreadful looking thing.'

Sad to say, no ceremony of bell, book and candle was

required to persuade the Clapham Road Ghost to stop holding up the traffic. Some genius discovered that the spooky phenomenon which would suddenly appear and just as suddenly fade away was caused by the way a street lamp was reflected in certain windows.

'I think in the end they moved the lamp,' said the former ghost watcher pensively. And that was the end of that.

Love and War at Southwold

SOUTHWOLD has a delightful old-fashioned charm and yet it has known great drama and excitement in the past, notably when much of the town was destroyed by fire in 1659, and in 1672 when the English fleet fought the Dutch in a fierce battle in Sole Bay.

If you visit Southwold today you may call at Sutherland House in the main street, now tea rooms, but at the time when Southwold teemed with sailors from the men of war anchored in the bay it was used as the headquarters of the High Admiral of the Fleet, James, Duke of York, and the Commander of the flagship, *Royal James*, Edward Montague, Earl of Sandwich.

The romantic story which has survived the centuries concerns the noble Earl and a certain red-haired maidservant aged 16. Apparently on the night before the fateful morning of the 28th May 1672, the Earl and his charming young companion spent their time in dalliance, and she deserted her attic room for the splendid first floor room allocated to the amorous Earl.

But all too soon duty called, and the story goes that the Earl overslept and arrived when the battle was already under way. It was a fierce engagement which raged till dark, the air thick with smoke from the Dutch fire ships, and the Earl of Sandwich acquitted himself valiantly in the midst of it until his ship fell foul of a fire ship and went up in flames.

They found the Earl's body a week later, and he lies in Westminster Abbey in Henry VII's Chapel.

One can imagine the little red-haired maid standing at the window of the Earl's bedroom, waiting in vain for a sight of her aristocratic lover who would never come. They say that when she finally accepted that her romance was over, she hanged herself.

There is a local legend that sometimes the little maid can still be seen at the window of the Earl's first floor bedroom. And the residents say that the sound of footsteps descending from the attic to the Earl's room have often been heard, and at times the bedclothes in this room are found disturbed, furniture moved and cushions scattered. And the most likely time for these supernatural happenings is annually on the eve of the anniversary of the Battle of Sole Bay.

IN Alasdair Alpin MacGregor's *Ghost Book* he writes that early one morning two men were walking down the path from Gun Hill, Southwold towards the sea when they passed a woman 'of great elegance and beauty' with a shawl over her head.

She was so striking in appearance that both instinctively turned to look after her and saw her disappear behind the Round House by the cliff edge. When they thought about it, they found it strange that she had been so conspicuous as it was not yet light, and wondered if there might be a ship in the harbour, and perhaps the lady might be the captain's wife.

They went down to the harbour and found a man struggling in the water and were able to rescue him. His boat had capsized and his two companions had drowned.

Was there some connection between seeing the beautiful ghost and happening to be in time to save a drowning man? Who can say, but this apparition has been seen at other times, and an acquaintance of MacGregor's, Miss Helen Palmer, told him that she too had seen the lady with the shawl over her head on Gun Hill, and described her as 'a gentle and reassuring apparition'.

GUN Hill with its six cannon overlooking the bay has another ghost, a figure that is seen standing beside one of the guns, and the local story has it that an unfortunate young soldier lost his head when one of the cannon exploded. The guns date back to 1745 when they were given to the town, and apparently because of their presence the Germans considered Southwold to be a fortified town, and bombed it in the First World War.

Glowing Gravestones

IN the churchyard at Lawshall, not so long ago, two young men walking home from the pub one night had an eerie experience. They noticed a gravestone which seemed to glow in the darkness. A friend of theirs was passing by at the time and noticed the two men and a third figure behind them whom she assumed was with them.

But next day when the two young men returned out of curiosity to have another look at the gravestone, although they remembered its position and had noticed that it was marked with a cross, there was no trace of it in the churchyard. And when their friend mentioned seeing them and their companion the night before, this just added to the mystery, since as far as they knew no one had been with them!

Oddly enough in February 1997 another gravestone began to glow at night, this time in the churchyard of Holy Trinity church at Wingate, Co Durham. It marked the grave of Corporal George Henry Longstaff, 18th Hussars, killed in action in March 1918.

The local vicar put the phenomenon down to a nearby security light, but the light's owner pointed out that the light had been in use for three years and the gravestone had only just begun to shine in the dark. Also, the security light only reacted to movement and was not on constantly.

No doubt there is a reasonable explanation for these strange happenings – isn't there?

Oulton Broad

FAMOUS 19th-century author George Borrow used to live at Oulton Broad in a house he called 'Lavengro' after his well-known work. There he wrote his books in an octagonal summerhouse by the water.

He was a great walker in his lifetime, and his striking figure, six foot three inches tall, was a familiar sight striding through the countryside in his Spanish cloak and large broad-brimmed hat, a long staff in his hand.

It is said that his ghost can still be seen around his old haunts and his gardener used to tell people that he often saw his former master enjoying a swim in the water near his home.

15

Supernatural Walberswick and Neighbourhood

WALBERSWICK is a pretty village which, like other places on the East Anglian coast, was once a busy port and for a time it reaped the benefit when violent storms over the years caused the silting up of Dunwich harbour. But Walberswick's good fortune was shortlived as ruinous fires and the perpetual erosion by the stormy sea stole its prosperity, and there was such poverty among the residents that at the end of the 17th century they could not afford to keep the church in repair. Today half of it remains a ruin.

Nonetheless Walberswick has great charm and is very appealing to artists. On a sunny day there is nothing to suggest that this is a place with more than its fair share of ghostly stories. But wander down to the river where the ferry runs between Walberswick and Southwold and, as the time for the last ferry of the day approaches, keep an eye open for an old man and a child apparently on their way to catch it.

This is a well-known story in the locality, repeated by Alasdair Alpin MacGregor in his *Ghost Book*. Apparently a visitor once passed the couple on his way to board the ferry, and when the ferryman showed every sign of setting off, he suggested that they waited as two more passengers were coming. Yet when he looked back there was now no trace of them. The ferryman gave him a look full of meaning.

'We never waits for them,' was all he said, but the visitor discovered that many local people were well aware of the manifestation, and some claimed to have themselves seen the two ghosts. Miss Helen Palmer, who had a number of paranormal experiences in Suffolk, told MacGregor that she, too, had more than once seen the old man holding a small boy by the hand when she was waiting for the ferry. The first time she drew the ferryman's attention to them, thinking he hadn't noticed, but was told 'They never cross'.

A reader's letter to the *East Anglian Magazine* in 1958 describes how during the ferry's last trip about two years previously she noticed a man and a boy watching the boat cross and wondered at the time how they could have walked past her without being noticed. As she looked 'a veil seemed to descend and they disappeared', and she heard later that they were the ghosts of a man and a boy who were drowned whilst crossing by the ferry.

Miss Helen Palmer also told MacGregor that she had been badly frightened by a monster which haunted the Green and the road between the Bell Inn and the vicarage. She said that her most terrifying experience occurred on a bright, sunny September morning when she was blackberrying on the Common. A cold wind suddenly sprang up and she distinctly heard the sound of galloping hooves growing louder and louder as they approached. 'I looked all around, but could see nothing except the rough grass, the bushes and the blue untroubled sky. Nonetheless I took to my heels and made for home.'

She told neighbours about it later and was advised that

they never crossed that particular bit of land as there was an 'evil haunt' on it.

As recounted in the Black Dog chapter, two other local ladies described to MacGregor how they had once actually seen 'the terrible monster of the Common'. Perhaps Black Shuck sometimes takes in Walberswick on his journey between Aldeburgh and Cromer? Dogs and horses appear to sense something here as they often seem to be frightened and refuse to go on, although there is nothing visible.

September 1879 saw the coming of the railway which ran from Halesworth to Southwold, taking in Wenhaston, Blythburgh and Walberswick. It is long gone now and where the old track ran is known as Dead Man's Gulley. This is apparently another area where horses shy nervously, and there are rumours that it is haunted. People walking along the track have heard a curious moaning sound hard to locate, sometimes described as the Walberswick Whisperers! There are vague stories of spectral appearances and suggestions that the railway track may have been built over an ancient burial ground. Whatever gives the area its eerie reputation, dogs and horses certainly seem aware of it.

Walberswick parish church also has its ghost, or ghosts, and a group of choristers at choir practice once saw a Victorian gentleman with what appeared to be a roll of paper under his arm.

On 27th July 1931 at about 5.20 pm Eric Blair (George Orwell the writer) was sitting outside the church when he noticed a 'small and stooping' man in brown walking along and going into the churchyard. Blair took him to be a workman, but then realised that as the man passed him there had been no sound at all. Out of curiosity he went into the churchyard but there was no one there or anywhere in sight. He wrote to a friend about the rather odd happening, and said that only about 20 seconds elapsed from the time he saw the man to finding the churchyard empty.

At nearby Blythburgh is the beautiful church known as the Cathedral of the Marshes which I always visit when I am in the area to see the magnificent angel roof — and the claw marks left after the legendary storm in 1577 when the Devil in the form of Black Shuck is said to have descended on the churches of Blythburgh and Bungay.

Blythburgh Common has a picnic area known as Toby's Walks, no doubt named after the black soldier, Tobias Gill, now believed to haunt there. Tobias was a drummer with troops stationed in the neighbourhood in 1754, and when the body of Anne Blakemore, a young local girl, was found dead on the common, he was accused of the crime and found guilty. He was hanged close to the scene of the murder and his body, after the gruesome custom of those days, was left to hang on a gibbet.

An old account says that Tobias's body hung there for nearly half a century until it fell to pieces. Not surprisingly, there is a ghost story which involves a phantom coach drawn by headless horses and the coachman is said to be the ghost of Tobias Gill.

In an article called 'These for Remembrance' by Eliza Vaughan she writes that a friend's grandfather was driving from the coast to his home in the village one night and he had three men in the cart with him. As he drew close to the gibbet near the old barn, he saw coming towards him a large coach drawn by four headless black horses, and driven by a headless coachman!

His three companions jumped from the cart in terror, but the driver stayed where he was and bravely drove straight at the apparition and went through it. He said afterwards that it felt like dashing through a cold fog!

There are several stories suggesting that isolated Westwood Lodge in Blythburgh is haunted, and in 1951 the *East Anglian Daily Times* reported the death of someone who had claimed to have seen one of the ghosts. Mr Andrew List used to regale his listeners with an account of the day he saw a ghostly horseman galloping by, thought to be John Brooke who lived at the Lodge from 1645 to 1652, a man believed to have been unpopular because of the way he treated his tenants.

Another Westwood Lodge story concerns the Lady in the Silver Dress. In October 1972 three brave young policemen visited the mansion on the edge of the marsh, which had been standing empty for ten years since the death of the last occupant. Intrigued by the story of the mysterious silver lady, often seen over the previous sixty years, the three men embarked on their first ghost hunt.

They knew that an old gamekeeper who still lived nearby professed to have seen the ghost several times, but had been so terrified that he would never go near the building at night. And the son of the present gamekeeper had reported a sighting only three days before the three intrepid ghost hunters arrived!

Well equipped with torches, candles, cotton, gummed tape and a tape recorder, they searched the house and taped cotton across doorways. Later at 1.20 am when they checked, they found that the cotton which had been firmly taped across the entrance to the hall was now displaced and hanging loose. And they knew that none of them was responsible as, after fixing it, they had remained together. Were they about to have an encounter of the supernatural kind?

They decided to remain in the hall to await events, and suddenly there was a dull thud from somewhere 'deep inside the house', and the room which had seemed quite warm appeared to be getting distinctly colder.

'The atmosphere was electric', said one of the young men, 'and although nothing could be seen, one had the impression that something was there.'

Several more deep thuds followed, one immediately overhead, and all three found themselves watching the staircase, convinced that something was about to appear. Once again they noticed that it was becoming increasingly cold, and although there was nothing to see, they were conscious of a presence. Then more thuds were heard, but the silver lady remained elusive and after a few minutes the room's temperature returned to normal.

Sadly during the rest of their time at the Lodge no silver lady rewarded their vigil, and as there were no further incidents, they left at 4 am.

The White Hart pub at Blythburgh stands by the side of the road, a handsome old place reputed to be haunted. The heavy oak door behind the bar leads to the living quarters and from time to time there is a knock which sounds 'as though the person who knocked wore a ring'. The building was once the meeting place of the Ecclesiastical Court and in her *Haunted East Anglia* Joan Forman suggests that the prior, head of the nearby religious settlement, would have worn a ring as part of his official insignia when, in the course of his duties, he visited the court from time to time.

The Queen's Head at nearby Blyford is close by the church and there were said to be passages linking the two which were well used in the old smuggling days, in fact one underground passage was discovered during structural alterations. A past landlord's wife saw four 'bluish lights' more than once in the bedroom which 'vanished through the wardrobe' and the landlord heard odd cracks and booming noises almost like an explosion. They both caught the sound of mysterious footsteps and once when the bar was full everyone there heard the sound of someone apparently walking about overhead. As it happened two off-duty policemen were present and, thinking the intruder might be a burglar, both of them rushed upstairs to investigate. But there was no one there and no sign of disturbance.

Tradition has it that the Queen's Head was once the headquarters of a gang of smugglers and it seems likely that echoes of the old inn's exciting past are still audible today for those with ears to hear them.

16

The City that Drowned

IT was summertime in the mid-1970s when a young man and his girl friend on holiday hitch-hiked into Dunwich. They spent a pleasant evening in the village pub and when they emerged it was still so mild and warm that they decided to curl up in their sleeping bags on the beach for the night.

They found a sheltered spot in a small cove just below the ruins of Greyfriars monastery and settled down to sleep, but it must have been in the early hours of the morning that something woke them. It was quite dark but still possible to see that the area of beach where they were was as empty as it had been when they arrived. The sounds they could hear, however, were unmistakably those of a group of children at play.

How long the children's voices continued they couldn't say. The sounds were not clearly identifiable as words, but both had no doubt about what they were hearing. And yet, how could a group of children be playing and chattering together in the dark in the early hours of the morning?

The two young people were overcome with sleep before either felt inclined to get up and investigate the mystery, but as the young man said later, 'That the sounds were made by village children at such an unearthly hour seems highly unlikely. I like to think what we really heard on that night we spent in the cove were the sounds of play made by the children of Dunwich before it slid into the sea.'

A place with Dunwich's long and stormy history is bound to have its ghosts and haunting memories. Walk down the quiet village street leading to the sea and you will see Dunwich Museum, with the charming little cream Dunwich rose blooming by the door in summer. Go inside and discover that this peaceful spot was once a great city, one of England's most prosperous and flourishing ports. At its peak during the time of Henry II the city covered almost a square mile, and was reputed to contain many churches, chapels and religious houses, hospitals, splendid buildings including a King's Palace, and a busy harbour full of merchant ships and the fishing fleet.

In his *Highways and Byways of East Anglia*, the historian W.A. Dutt likens the Dunwich of long ago to mysterious and romantic Atlantis and the lost land of Lyonesse. Looking at the bleak stretch of beach beneath the crumbling cliffs it is difficult to believe that the whole bustling world that was Dunwich has vanished beneath the sea, leaving so little evidence that it ever existed.

But echoes remain. Great storms over the centuries brought the sea surging into the city and Dunwich fought a losing battle as its buildings were swept away and its harbour blocked with tons of sand and shingle. One of the most famous local legends is that sometimes the bells of the submerged churches can still be heard, ringing beneath the waves. It used to be said that sailors and fishermen would not put to sea when they heard the bells as it was a sure sign of a coming storm. The curious thing is that the peal of the phantom bells could be recognised because one note of the carillon was missing!

The ruins of Greyfriars monastery stand in the fields close by the cliff top. Local people say this is a haunted place where mysterious lights sometimes glow amid the ruins, shadowy monks still go about their affairs, and the chanting of ghostly voices still floats on the air.

The woodland close by has a strange atmosphere. It is so silent and still that one wanders the path down to the fenced off cliff edge half expecting to meet someone or something. According to Anthony Hippisley Coxe's *Haunted Britain*, in Victorian times a brother of the Lord of the Manor of Sotterly Hall fell in love with a young maid employed at the house called Grey Friars. This was a romance never destined to have a happy ending and, forbidden to meet his love, the young man died of a broken heart. His ghost is said to walk the path through the woods near Grey Friars, a shooting box in Victorian times. Another ghost said to roam this area is the Victorian squire himself mounted on an Arab thoroughbred horse.

Visitors to Dunwich looking out over the North Sea can give their imagination full rein, picturing a ghost city of sunken buildings now home to a variety of sea creatures. And in recent times there have been underwater expeditions by divers to search for the ruins of the lost world of Dunwich.

Visibility in the rough waters of the North Sea is poor and some of the ruins are submerged in sand and mud on the sea bed. One can easily imagine the eerie atmosphere that the divers encounter and when the ruins of St Peter's church were discovered in 1973 after a long search, the diver's elation at his success was overshadowed by the chilling impression that someone or something was beside him in the darkness. Other divers, too, have had the odd sensation that they were not alone, although at the time no other diver was present.

Dunwich is a place of memories and legends. Do the bells of those submerged churches still ring, or is it just a phantom echo? And what of the shadowy figures sometimes seen by the shore? And the laughter of children of long ago that a young couple heard one summer night?

There is an ancient legend that three holy crowns were once buried in East Anglia to protect England from invasion. One was unearthed at Rendlesham in the 18th century, and one was believed to be located at Dunwich, and the third has never been found. The Dunwich crown obviously failed to prevent the invasion of the sea and may now lie with the ruins of that once great city beneath the wild North Sea.

17

Murder on the Mayfly

THERE is something eerily romantic about phantom ships, strange visions which sail into view only to vanish like sea mist into nothing. Most people have heard of the legendary *Flying Dutchman* and wondered if the amazing story can possibly be any more than that, a legend. And yet there is a straightforward report of one of many sightings, this one made by none other than King George V when he was Prince George, a 16 year old midshipman on board the British warship *Inconstant* on 11th July 1881.

It was 4 am when what he described as 'a phantom ship all aglow' crossed their bows, emitting a strange phosphorescent light which brightly lit up another boat 200 yards away. All this was also seen by thirteen other crew on board the *Inconstant,* and two other ships, and other sightings have been reported around the Cape of Good Hope where the *Flying Dutchman* is believed to have vanished in the 17th century.

Suffolk, too, has its phantom vessel story – of the ghostly wherry *Mayfly,* cursed for ever to return to Oulton Broad every 24th June at around 12.30 am with its cargo of lost souls, searching for an anchorage it can never find.

At the time of the *Mayfly*'s tragic voyage in 1851 the skipper was a man known as 'Blood' Stephenson, a nickname recognised and feared in many parts of the world, but not by the owners of the wherry, who accepted him as a master mariner well qualified to captain the huge vessel.

For some time all went well with the *Mayfly*, delivering goods between Beccles and Yarmouth, mostly grain. But in June 1851 it had a more interesting cargo, a chest containing a large amount of gold which the owners were sending to the bank at Yarmouth in the care of Captain Stephenson, as they believed it would travel more safely than if it was exposed to the dangers of the road.

A more reckless undertaking it would be hard to imagine in view of Stephenson's unsavoury history, compounded by the fact that the daughter of Mr Downey, one of the owners, went along too. In order to divert any unwelcome interest when the money was loaded on the ship, the plan was that 17 year old Millicent should appear to be off to stay with a relative in Yarmouth, and the large trunk on board would obviously be assumed to be her luggage.

'Blood' Stephenson must have thought it was his lucky day. Now all he had to do was dispose of his crew, consisting of the mate, a deckhand and a boy, and then it was away to foreign parts with his haul of gold and pretty young Millicent too!

For a time the *Mayfly* sailed along the river Waveney as usual, until the Captain called the mate to him, and gave him an idea of his plans. The mate did not hide his shocked dismay at this unexpected turn of events but he scarcely had time to protest before Stephenson sprang upon him, and after a fierce struggle, stunned by Stephenson's onslaught, he was thrown overboard to drown.

Beyond Yarmouth, wind filling the sails, Stephenson turned the *Mayfly* towards the open sea and, noticing a change in the motion of the boat, Millicent came on deck. Stephenson reassured her by saying that they were just taking a little sea cruise en route. But by the next day when she asked about turning for home, Stephenson announced that they were never going back to Yarmouth. The *Mayfly* and everything on board was now his, and he intended that Millicent should become his wife.

If Stephenson had expected this news to be received with enthusiasm, he had underestimated Millicent. 'You mean you are stealing the ship, and the money?' she cried angrily, her face white with terror.

Stephenson was in no mood to argue. He grabbed the frightened girl and dragged her below to the cabin, and the two members of the crew heard screaming and crying but dared not interfere. Later Millicent appeared on deck, pursued by the Captain. She was bleeding from a cut on her neck, and with belated chivalry the deckhand rushed forward to intercept Stephenson. Backwards and forwards across the deck the two men fought, until finally the Captain caught the other man off guard, and landed a knockout blow to his jaw. Before he could regain consciousness, Stephenson seized his body and threw him overboard into the sea.

Bert the boy, who had watched in horror, now rushed forward to do what he could to help Millicent, only to see Stephenson fall dead at her feet, a knife in his heart. Somehow the frightened girl had found the weapon and the strength to kill her powerful assailant, but it had all been too much. As Bert reached her, she gave a piercing scream and fell dead across the Captain's body.

Bert, stunned by these horrendous events, found himself alone on a ship he had no idea how to control, with two dead bodies on deck. When daylight came he loaded the dinghy with provisions and climbed in, leaving the *Mayfly* with her awful cargo to sail away.

He was rescued by a passing ship, but once ashore Bert

was ill for a long time in a Plymouth hospital until he recovered sufficiently to send for the owner of the *Mayfly* and tell his horrifying story.

One night some time later when Bert and Mr Downey were fishing on Oulton Broad they noticed how oppressive the atmosphere had become, with a sickening sulphurous smell in the air. Then, to their amazement, they saw a ship in full sail approaching and recognised the *Mayfly*, now a white ghost ship gleaming with phosphorescence, and as she raced by they saw a skeleton at the wheel and the screaming figure of Millicent pursued by 'Blood' Stephenson on deck re-enacting that terrible night which ended in their deaths. It was too much for Millicent's poor father who died of shock.

That was the 24th June, three years after the *Mayfly's* disastrous voyage, and since then the wherry is said to return annually to Oulton Broad, ploughing her way through the moored boats but leaving them undamaged as she continues her never-ending journey with murder on deck and death at the helm.

Can such a melodramatic story be true? Dr Charles Sampson's collection of *Ghosts of the Broads*, published in 1931, includes the saga of the *Mayfly* and he mentions various psychical societies who have investigated the story, and the attempts that have been made to record the wherry's annual visit by special cameras. But there seems to have been no further news in recent years. Local newspapers have recalled the tragic story from time to time but no one appears to have come forward with a thrilling eye witness account. Has the ghost wherry *Mayfly* finally made port? Shall we ever know?

18

Strange Discoveries

THORINGTON Hall is a splendid gabled house with a high six-stacked cluster chimney at Stoke by Nayland, and it has been in the possession of the National Trust since 1941.

It is said to be always cold there, even in summertime, although this does not necessarily have anything to do with the ghost who haunts one of the upstairs passages. They call her the Brown Lady, as she wears a brown garment tied round the waist with a cord.

When Fred and Elizabeth Burton came to the Hall as caretakers just before the last war, they noticed the unexplained sound of footsteps at night but soon got used to them. However, one evening when Mrs Burton was away, her husband was going round the building attending to the wartime blackout and as he climbed the stairs he saw a figure in an old-fashioned brown dress standing at the top. She raised her hand to her mouth as if in surprise at his presence, then turned and vanished.

That was the only time the Brown Lady was seen when the Burtons lived at Thorington Hall, but one day they noticed their dog up on the landing wagging his tail and jumping up as if he was greeting someone, but there was no one there.

From time to time heavy footsteps have been heard in various parts of the house, and once in more recent years a visitor woke in the night and sensed the presence of someone in the room, but she said it was not a frightening experience.

In 1937 during restoration a lady's shoe was found behind the ornamental plasterwork. It is now in Colchester Museum where it was identified as 16th century. It is a superstition dating back many hundreds of years that shoes hidden in buildings will ward off evil and bring good luck. June Swann, former keeper of the boot and shoe collection at Northampton Museum and a world authority on historic footwear, says that the walling in of shoes was intended as a protection, and they were placed to guard all the entry points of a building, the doors, windows, chimneys and roof.

Other forms of protection for a building sometimes used an animal, or the skull of a wolf, dog, ox or horse as a foundation offering. The Norman builders of Bury St Edmunds' Abbey are said to have placed the skulls of wolves beneath the gatehouse tower and forty horse skulls were found beneath the floor of a 17th-century house in Bungay.

During structural alterations to some 17th-century cottages at Fakenham Major, mummified cats were found in the roof space, and another cat and two kittens in the walls. The foreman, intrigued by such a curious find, took the cats home to show his wife, but at once odd things began to happen such as unexplained noises and tapping on the doors. Also, at the cottages where the builders were working they noticed a strange atmosphere building up which they found unnerving. Then footsteps were heard on the gravel drive when no one was there, and the men heard more footsteps overhead although they had just removed the ceiling! Obviously it was time to put everything back where they found it!

A similar story comes from Sudbury when an old watermill was being rebuilt for use as a hotel in 1971. A mummified cat was discovered in the roof and removed by the builder. A short time afterwards a financial crisis held up the work, and meanwhile a beam in the roof where the cat had been found broke and caused a great deal of damage.

The cat had been taken to a studio which was then mysteriously set on fire, although the cat was unscathed. It was removed to a farmhouse at Wickham St Paul, which also suffered a fire and, not surprisingly, the hotel owners then decided to re-inter the cat where it had originally been found.

This was done with due ceremony and a note apologising for disturbing the cat was included. And, after that, all was well.

19

Monks in the Market

ALTHOUGH ghosts come in great variety, one kind of apparition, especially in Suffolk, is by far the most persistent. I am talking about monks, but considering the number of ancient monasteries and priories there used to be and the great Abbey of Bury St Edmunds itself, perhaps it is not so surprising that some of the inhabitants still linger.

The Butter Market at Ipswich has seen many changes since an old monastery stood in the area, and a factory belonging to W.S. Cowell and Company which was built over the ruins has, in its turn, given place to the new shopping mall.

But during W.S. Cowell's time, the workers there had good reason to know that not every trace of the old monastery had gone. On at least two occasions young women employees looked up from their work to see an old monk standing there watching them, and promptly fainted from the shock.

And an Irish labourer working one night in the factory had a similar experience. He broke out in a cold sweat and stood there petrified with fright when he saw the ghostly figure of a monk slowly gliding towards him. But the figure never reached him. As it vanished into thin air a few feet in front of him, he let out a terrified yell and ran out of the building as fast as his wobbly legs would carry him. And nothing would persuade him to go back, even to collect his wages!

But long-term workers became used to supernatural sightings over the years. Sometimes footsteps would be heard when no one was there, and sometimes shadowy forms were seen in and around the factory.

One day an employee noticed a steel door set flush with the floor in a part of the building unfamiliar to him, and feeling curious he prised it open to reveal a flight of stone steps. It was obvious that the trapdoor had not been opened for a considerable time and, still curious, the man went down the steps which he found led to a tunnel, but a few yards along it had been sealed off leaving the mystery of where it led unsolved. It seems likely that it was part of the old monastery buildings.

On a slightly more macabre note, I was told that during some building work a sealed underground chamber was discovered, and when it was opened a number of skeletons were revealed. Was it some kind of charnel house? What was the secret behind their incarceration in this mysterious sealed chamber? Could they have been something to do with the old monastery? One's imagination suggests all kinds of grim scenarios which could perhaps throw some light on a reason for the subsequent hauntings.

There was apparently another interesting discovery when workmen were clearing the site before the new shopping mall was built. They came across an ancient deep well believed to date back to the monastery but apparently this intriguing find was not investigated. It was merely filled in. Remembering that at the time of the Dissolution of the Monasteries valuables may sometimes have been hurriedly hidden in wells one wonders what may still lie under the feet of Ipswich's shoppers.

Perhaps that is why those shadowy monks still lingered after Cowell's factory was built over the site of their monastery. And are perhaps still lingering even now?

20

Do You Believe in Fairises?

NO, its not a misprint. I do mean Fairises, or Fairisees, or even Ferishers, all East Anglian words for fairies. And if there are so many words for the little people, surely they must have existed and maybe still do. While I was finishing this book in the early months of 1998, a film was showing in cinemas throughout the country, based on the famous case of the Cottingley Fairies, and people were flocking to a London exhibition of Victorian fairy pictures. Peter Pan would have been pleased with us – perhaps we do believe in fairies!

In his *East Anglian Magic* book Nigel Pennick records that in the *Ipswich Journal* in 1877 there was a story about some Suffolk Ferishers at Bury St Edmunds, described as being as big as mice, wearing blue coats, yellow trousers and red caps.

And in Tavern Street, Stowmarket in the 19th century, local people gathered to secretly watch the Ferishers dance. They had sandy hair and pale complexions and if you annoyed them sparks would appear alarmingly beneath your feet.

I found a number of fairy sightings when I was writing my *Ghosts of Essex* book, and as one concerned Capel St Mary, just over the Essex border into Suffolk, I am repeating it here.

A London barrister had bought a run-down, semi-derelict house beside woodland on the fringe of Capel St Mary with the idea of renovating and restoring it to a habitable condition to make a home for his family.

One weekend he had travelled down there ahead of his wife and children, hoping to finish some work on the house before the family arrived next day. He was quite late going to bed, but woke to hear his name being called. He got up and went downstairs thinking that perhaps his family had arrived early after all, but there was no one waiting outside, so feeling puzzled he went back upstairs.

In the ceiling of his bedroom he had left a trapdoor open where he had been working earlier, and as he glanced up he was amazed to see a tiny man sitting on the edge of the opening, happily swinging his little legs to and fro. He was about two feet tall, dressed in a green shirt, brown leather breeches with braces, long stockings and boots, with a small trilby type hat perched on his head. The barrister stared incredulously at this unlikely sight, and for a brief period the little man stared back, and then abruptly vanished!

A friend who knows the barrister well told me that he is not the type of man to make up a story like this. Strange as it seems, he swore that he really had seen what appeared to be a fairybook brownie or goblin. And there was more. When he made a few discreet enquiries in the neighbourhood, he found that previous occupants of the house had reported sightings of fairies and goblins both indoors and out, but as the locals thought them rather an odd lot, no one had believed their stories!

And at Lawford, just over the border into Essex, in 1976 a resident had a delightful surprise as she walked down her garden path and was confronted by a tiny figure about a foot high. It was a quaintly dressed little old lady wearing a shawl and bonnet and tiny buttoned boots. She had a small posy of flowers in her hand, and both ladies stood for a while, eyeing each other somewhat nonplussed, then with a smile the fairy figure rose into the air like a miniature Mary Poppins and slowly floated away, graciously waving goodbye as she went!

In her *Haunted East Anglia* Joan Forman refers to the experience of an Ipswich man when he lived in Saxmundham as a child. He and his younger brother were on their way to Carlton Park to play one morning when, passing some meadowland along Harper's Lane, they were astonished to see a group of seven or eight figures dancing in a circle in the meadow about thirty yards away.

They were draped in filmy garments of white luminous muslin as they danced gracefully in 'a kind of follow-my-leader in a circle'. The little boys watched this unexpected sight for a few seconds until the dancing figures suddenly disappeared, and the lads went on their way, but apparently didn't tell anyone what they had seen until much later. Although now grown-up they have never forgotten what they saw.

Joan Forman refers to the 'dancing ghosts' but I suppose they could equally have been fairies, who are not necessarily small.

Fairies are notoriously capricious and need to be treated with respect, and forms of protection are to fill your pockets full of bread and to wear a daisy chain, the symbol of Phoebe, the sun goddess, which will ward off any of the little people bent on mischief. So now you know what to do, don't you?

21

Haunted Inns

From Badingham to Wickham Market

THE ghost hunter often finds that one story leads to another, and one May morning in 1997 during lunch at the White Horse Inn at Badingham, I was chatting to the son of the house, Scott Doughty.

This pleasant little pub, once a farmhouse dating back to the 14th century, doubles as the post office for the village, and Scott told me that it is said to be haunted. 'When I am in here alone at night I get an impression of someone walking through the bar,' he told me. 'I don't see anything, I just sense it.'

However, he had a much more interesting tale to tell about the White Hart at Wickham Market which his family used to keep. 'It was very haunted,' he said. His father insists he doesn't believe in ghosts, but one day he saw a figure pass through the bar. It was a woman wearing a sort of sackcloth dress.

Visitors never liked to stay in Room 14, said Scott, because odd things happened. Some described seeing a curious manifestation like the colours of the rainbow, and others thought they saw a cat lying on a seat in the room, but suddenly there was nothing there.

We drove on to Wickham Market and found that the large impressive White Hart building still had its inn sign, but was now used as shops, offices, and flats. When I made enquiries at the offices the Secretary, Sally Nelson, told me that oddly enough she had recently remarked to the only other person working in the office with her that she was convinced the building was haunted. When her colleague is away the answering machine is continually switching on for no reason. 'I expect its a fault on the line, but it never ever happens when he is here,' she said.

In a feature about haunted Suffolk pubs in the *East Anglian Daily Times* in 1981, it was reported that the White Hart was haunted by Betty Price who was the landlady there in the 18th century. Betty, it appears, was convicted of witchcraft and duly paid for her sins with her life.

The landlady of the time said that they sometimes heard creaks and groans in the early hours, and added that they had a chef who refused to go down to the staff cottages on his own. He was convinced that there was something supernatural down there.

So is an 18th-century witch playing with the answering machine, and was she the figure in sackcloth seen in the bar? And what of the mysterious ghost cat in Room 14? As that chef once said, it seems as if there is still something there.

Melton's Horse and Groom ... and Cat

ANOTHER pub with a supernatural feline is the Horse and Groom at Melton, just outside Woodbridge. Towards the end of the 1970s a young American stayed in the pub for several weeks. One day he asked if the landlady had recently bought a cat, as several times he had felt there was a cat in the room although he hadn't actually seen it.

There was no cat at the pub, but a few days later he came down to the bar looking distressed and said he had woken in the night to find a very large cat lying across his throat. He jumped up and the cat leapt towards the closed window, and disappeared through it! A few nights later he was heard calling out in the night, and said the same thing had happened again, and he was moved to a different room for the rest of his stay.

Some time later, in November 1978, a group of RAF men stayed in the pub during a NATO exercise and two of them slept in Room 3, the same room the American visitor had used. Next morning they came down and asked if in future the cat could be shut in the kitchen at night. Apparently one of them had woken in the night to find a cat lying across his throat, and when he moved it had jumped off and vanished.

The Horse and Groom also claims a white lady wearing a shroud-like garment who patrols an upstairs corridor and has been known to frighten sleepers who wake to find her standing by the bed!

One landlord said that sometimes when he was downstairs in the bar he would hear the sound of the television upstairs, but when he went up to turn it off he found it was already off, just as he had left it. But when he went back downstairs, the same noise would begin again.

'It gets a bit eerie here at times,' he admitted.

The Swan at Lavenham

L AVENHAM still retains the unspoilt look of a medieval wool town with its beautiful timbered houses and ancient Guildhall now owned by the National Trust. At the junction of Water Street and Church Street stands the impressive Swan Inn with its decorative pargeting showing the Tudor rose and the fleur de lys. The 15th-century gabled Wool Hall was incorporated into the Swan about twenty-five years ago.

Room 15 at the Swan is reputed to be haunted by the wrath of an under housekeeper who, becoming depressed when a colleague was promoted above her, committed suicide by hanging herself.

Sponsored Hallowe'en vigils have taken place there for charity, and in 1991 a security guard had the fright of his life when he encountered the ghost. Not surprisingly, none of the staff like to be in the vicinity of the haunted room after nightfall.

A Restless Ghost at Long Melford

THE large timber-framed Bull at Long Melford was built in 1450 as a rich wool merchant's mansion, and later, in the 16th century, became an inn. There is a courtyard at the back with part of a gallery dating back to its days as a posting house.

The Bull has long been a target for ghost hunters, its haunting supposedly dating back to the murder in 1648 of a yeoman farmer, Richard Everard, who was stabbed by Roger Greene in the hallway of the inn. The motive which lay behind it is unknown, and Roger Greene went to the gallows for his crime. There was even more mystery surrounding the affair, as the body of the murdered man was laid out in the lounge of the hotel, but by morning it had vanished! Rumour has it that Everard's grave in the churchyard has never contained a body but this leaves even more questions. Did Everard's body turn up again? If not, why was an empty coffin buried?

Not surprisingly, Everard's ghost is restless, and the heavy old oak door which leads from the hall to the dining room has been seen to swing open of its own accord on many occasions.

Poltergeist-type phenomena were particularly prevalent

118

here in the 1970s when objects were seen to fly through the air and the chairs in the dining room were sometimes moved from their usual position and found in the morning grouped cosily round the fireplace. Colonel Dawson, the landlord at that time, heard footsteps pass his bedroom door one night when he was alone in the inn, but when he looked out there was no one there. He brought his dogs upstairs but as soon as they reached the corridor outside his bedroom they became terrified and refused to go any further.

A visitor also heard footsteps outside early one morning, and a knock on her door. She called 'Come in', thinking it was the maid with her morning tea, but immediately after there was a loud crash as though the tray with the tea things had been dropped. She got up and opened the door expecting to find broken crockery, but there was no one there and nothing to account for the noise she had heard.

Although the Bull at Long Melford is always included in any book of haunted inns, ghostly activity seems to have subsided in recent times.

Strange Happenings at Bildeston

THE Crown Inn at Bildeston is another hostelry dating back to the prosperous days of the wool trade for it was built in 1495 as a home for a wealthy wool merchant. It is a superb old timbered building, long reputed to be haunted by the sound of mysterious footsteps and unexplained hammering or knocking noises. A more alarming happening has been reported by people who have felt the touch of icy fingers!

A maidservant is said to have hanged herself, and now in the form of a grey lady haunts the courtyard and the stable where she took her own life. A figure wearing a three-cornered hat has been seen sitting quietly in the lounge bar and once a barman went to remind him that it was closing time only to see him vanish before his eyes. And two Victorian children holding a musical box have been seen sometimes wandering round the inn.

On one occasion a customer returned to the bar looking white and scared. He said he had been about to enter the gents in the courtyard when someone opened the door for him, but when he went in there was no one else there.

The famous clairvoyant Tom Corbett visited the Crown in the 1960s and confirmed that there was a psychic atmosphere in the place. In the light of all the strange happenings reported there, I rather think he was right.

22

The Unknown Bride

L AWFORD Church stands on a hill above the river Stour on the border between Essex and Suffolk. Inside the building there are many stone carvings of creatures of the countryside such as squirrels and owls and two delightful and unusual 'chains' of little men dancing, wrestling and playing musical instruments, each figure holding onto the leg of his neighbour above.

This was one of the churches featured in a programme on Anglia Television a few years ago presented by John Timpson. There are several ghost stories associated with the church and in the programme Edna Simms, who has lived in Lawford most of her life, recounted an uncanny experience she had when she was a young girl in the last war.

She was walking home through the churchyard one winter evening when she was surprised to notice flickering lights shining through the church windows. She went up to the door and opened it and at once noticed a smell of incense, and then she saw walking down the aisle a line of monks, swinging their incense burners and chanting as they came.

As the shadowy scene faded Edna gently closed the church door and next day when she met the Rector, she told him what she had seen. 'You realise what you saw don't you?' he said. 'Yesterday was All Souls Day, and you went back in time and saw the monks of the old days.'

Edna is particularly sensitive to the paranormal, and I hoped she might be able to tell me more about a Lawford story which I found particularly interesting. This is the strange case of the extra bride. On several occasions when a wedding group has been photographed outside the church, when the picture is developed another 'unknown' bride is seen standing behind the real bride. Who is she, and how can this have happened?

When I asked Edna Simms about it, she told me that she had actually seen the bride ghost many years ago when she was a young girl of thirteen. 'I was coming home across the park in the dusk,' she said, 'when I felt as if there was someone behind me. I turned round and there standing at the church gate was the ghost bride dressed in white with a very heavy white veil over her face. Then as I looked she turned round and disappeared.'

Next day at school Edna's teacher said that she had seen a wedding photograph which showed the ghostly bride standing behind the real one.

'The story is that on her wedding day the bride was at the church waiting for her groom when the best man arrived with terrible news,' said Edna. 'As the bridegroom was riding to the church his horse had suddenly bolted, throwing him to the ground, and he had been killed. In her grief, the bride ran to her father's grave in the church-yard, where she cried herself to death.'

Edna has seen three wedding photographs which show the ghostly extra bride, the last one being twenty-one years ago. I have also heard that many times a phantom bride, her veil streaming behind her, has been seen running from the church door through the churchyard. Is this a shadowy replay of the tragic day when a broken-hearted bride, told that her groom had met his death on the way to their wedding, ran from the church to fling herself on her father's grave? Or is it yet another bride? There seems to be nothing else known that could account for it.

The only other story remotely similar that I know is told in my *Ghosts of Hertfordshire* book. The dower house to the Gorhambury estate at St Albans is called The Pre and in the 19th century was occupied by the Toulmin family, Henry and Emma and their fourteen children. Many years later the house became an hotel where wedding receptions took place, and the lovely garden leading down to the river Ver was a favourite place for photographs. Occasionally when the pictures of the bride and groom were developed, something odd appeared. There beside the bridal pair stood the shadowy figure of a child. A member of the staff of those days recalled the first time it happened.

'The young couple had posed on the lawn just below Room 15', she said, 'and when the photograph was developed there was this extraordinary outline of a small child. No one could explain it. There were no children in the wedding party or among the guests at the hotel.' Subsequently the same little figure appeared on other wedding photographs, usually in the month of August.

When Isobel Toulmin, the youngest of the Toulmin children, was an old lady in her nineties she heard about this, and said she was convinced that she was the shadowy child in the pictures. 'If there is a powerful affection for a place, I am sure a living person can project the ghost of their earlier self,' she said, explaining that she never liked strangers on the lawn in the garden she had loved so much.

Many apparitions seem to be due to some past event powerful enough to leave an impression on the surroundings which may become apparent in certain conditions. But the appearance of a ghost on a photograph is a rare event and both these cases are mysterious and hard to explain.

Index

Aldeburgh 52
Ancient House 13–18
Archer, Fred 81–82

Babes in the Wood 70
Badingham 115
Balls, William 22
Balsham 53
Barnby 42, 43
Barsham Marshes 44
Barton Turf 48
Battle of Sole Bay 88
Beccles 42, 43, 103
Bigod, Hugh 72
Bildeston 119
Black Shuck 50–54, 93, 94
Blakemore, Anne 94
Blundeston 22
Blyford 96
Blythburgh 53, 67, 93–96
Blythburgh Common
    44–45
Boxford 52
Bradfield St George
    23–29
Brooke, John 95
Brown Lady, The 106
Bull, The 118–119
Bullard, John 64
Bungay 51, 53, 72, 107

Bury St Edmunds 23, 34,
    37, 41, 61–63, 112
Bury St Edmunds Abbey
    61–62, 107, 109
Butter Market, The
    109–110

Capel St Mary 112–113
Cathedral of the Marshes
    94
Charles II 17
Christchurch Mansion
    85–86
Clapham Road Ghost
    86–87
Colley, Thomas 67
Corbett, Tom 120
Corder, William 31–36,
    37–41
Corton 22
Cottingley Fairies 112
Covehithe 75
Cowell & Co., W.S.
    109–110
Cromer 52
Crown Inn, The 119–120
Cupola House Hotel 62

de Calne, Richard 69, 70,
    71

de Gladville, Bartholomew 73
Ditchingham 51
Dobbs, 'Brainy' 58
Dobbs, John 58
Dunwich 98–101

Everard, Richard 118

Fairises or fairies 112–114
Fakenham Major 107
Felixstowe 55
Ferishers 112–114
Fornham St Martin 70, 72

George V 102
Gill, Tobias 94
Great Bealings House 76–80
Green Children, The 68–72
Greene, Roger 118
Grey Friars 100
Greyfriars Monastery 98, 100
Gubblecote Cross 67
Gun Hill 89
Gypsy's Grave, The 82

Halesworth 93
Henry II 72
Hopkins, Matthew 16
Hopton 19–22
Horse and Groom, The 116–117

Ipswich 13–18, 55, 85, 86, 109

Johnson, William 46

Kentford 82
Kesgrave 58
Kessingland 44, 73–75
Kessingland Serpent 73–75

Lakeland, Mary 13–18
Lakenheath 43
Lakenheath Air Force Base 55
Langham 59
Lavenham 117–118
Lawford 113, 121–122
Lawshall 89
Leiston 51
Letheringham Watermill 64–65
Long Marston 67
Long Melford 118–119
Lound 22
Lowestoft 19–22, 42, 86–87

Marten, Maria 30–36, 37
Martlesham Heath, RAF 57–59
Mayfly 102–105
Melton 116
Middleton 52

Montague, Edward 87–88
Moyses Hall Museum 35
Nelson, Henrietta 46–49
Newmarket 81–82
Nutshell, The 62

Orford Castle 72, 73
Oulton Broad 90, 102, 105

Parham 59–60
Polstead 36, 82–85
Polstead Rectory 82–85
Potsford 65–66
Priory Hotel 62

Queen's Head, The 96–97

Ralph, Abbot of
  Coggleshall 68, 72
Red Barn, The 30–36, 37
Rendlesham 101
Reydon Hall 52
Rider Haggard, Henry 74
Roos Hall 43–44
Rougham 23–29

Saxmundham 114
Shug Monkey 53
Smallburgh 48
Snell, Jonah 64–66
Sole Bay 87
Sotterly Hall 100
Southwold 52, 87–89, 91,
  93

Stephenson, 'Blood'
  102–105
Stoke by Nayland 106
Stowmarket 112
Suffolk Hotel, The 63
Sudbury 107–108
Sutherland House 87
Swan, The 117–118

Theatre Royal, The 63
Thorington Hall 106–107
Toby's Walks 94

Walberswick 44, 91–94
Walberswick Ferry 91
Walberswick Marsh 52
Walberswick Whisperers
  94
Wenhaston 93
West Suffolk Hospital 35,
  37
Westwood Lodge 95–96
West Wratting 53
White Hart, The
  (Blythburgh) 96
White Hart, The
  (Wickham Market)
  115–116
White Horse Inn 115
Wicken Fen 52
Wickham Market 65,
  115–116
Wickham St Paul 108

Wilkins, William 63
William of Newburgh 68
Woodbridge 76, 78
Woolpit 68

Yarmouth 103
Yaxley Hall 46, 49